I0820847

VIETNAM

BY LIZ SONNEBORN

Essential Library
An Imprint of Abdo Publishing
abdobooks.com

ABDOBOOKS.COM
Published by Abdo Publishing, a division of ABDO, PO Box 398166, Minneapolis, Minnesota 55439.

Printed in the United States of America, North Mankato, Minnesota.
052025
092025

Cover Photo: Shutterstock Images (waterfall, pattern)
Interior Photos: Shutterstock Images, 4–5, 8, 13, 14–15, 19 (globe), 26–27, 32, 33, 36–37, 42, 50, 52–53, 56, 70, 71, 80, 83, 87, 97, 101; Bunwit Unseree/Shutterstock Images, 7; Huy Thoai/Shutterstock Images, 16–17, 18; Red Line Editorial, 19 (map); Nhac Nguyen/AFP/Getty Images, 22–23, 25, 54, 94; Brown Bear/Windmill Books/Universal Images Group/Getty Images, 28; Tzido Sun/Shutterstock Images, 31; David Henley/Pictures from History/Universal Images Group/Getty Images, 39; Album/Alamy, 40; Bettmann/Getty Images, 45; Tim Page/Corbis Historical/Getty Images, 46; Alex Bowie/Hulton Archive/Getty Images, 49; David Parker/Alamy, 57; Alena Kolackova/Shutterstock Images, 60; Ulf Andersen/Getty Images Entertainment/Getty Images, 61; Adam Pretty/Hulton Archive/Getty Images, 64; Godong/Universal Images Group/Getty Images, 66–67; Yin Bogu/Xinhua News Agency/Getty Images, 68–69; STR/AFP/Getty Images, 72; Dang Anh/AFP/Getty Images, 76; Hien Phung Thu/Shutterstock Images, 78–79, 84; Jesus Salas Dual/Shutterstock Images, 88–89; Dragon Images/Shutterstock Images, 90; Sirisak Baokaew/Shutterstock Images, 93; Linh Pham/Getty Images News/Getty Images, 98–99

Editor: Marie Pearson
Series Designer: Maggie Villaume

Library of Congress Control Number: 2024948602

PUBLISHER'S CATALOGING-IN-PUBLICATION DATA
Names: Sonneborn, Liz, author.
Title: Vietnam / by Liz Sonneborn
Description: Minneapolis, Minnesota: Abdo Publishing, 2026 | Series: Essential library of countries | Includes online resources and index.
Identifiers: ISBN 9781098297060 (lib. bdg.) | ISBN 9798384919582 (ebook)
Subjects: LCSH: Geography--Juvenile literature. | Vietnam--Civilization--Juvenile literature. | Asia--Juvenile literature. | Vietnam--History--Juvenile literature.
Classification: DDC 959.7--dc23

CONTENTS

CHAPTER **ONE**

A TOUR OF VIETNAM

Fourteen-year-old Mia wakes up suddenly as she feels her grandmother nudge her shoulder. Grandma whispers that they are almost there. Mia looks out the airplane window. As the plane descends, the green countryside gives way to a cityscape of tall buildings and roads crowded with cars and motorbikes.

The trip from San Francisco, California, was long. Grandma, Mia, and Mia's mother, Amy, had taken a flight to Japan before boarding this airplane to their destination. After almost 20 hours, they finally arrive in Hanoi, the capital of Vietnam.[1] After Grandma and Grandpa retired, they began taking annual trips to Vietnam, the country where they were born and raised.

Hanoi covers about 1,205 square miles (3,120 sq km). It contains more than 60 parks and flower gardens.

This year, Grandpa hadn't felt up to it, so Grandma decided to treat Amy and Mia to a vacation there. Mia's grandparents had lived in California since 1978, but when they talked about Vietnam, they sometimes still called it their country.

Before leaving, Amy showed Mia Vietnam's location on a map. Mia saw that it was in Southeast Asia, just south of China. Snaking along the western edge of the South China Sea, Vietnam is a long, narrow country. As Mia traced it with her finger, she said it looked a little like the letter S. Their plan was to start in Hanoi in the north and move south, taking a few short plane rides to see some sights along the way.

CHILDREN OF THE DRAGON

According to Vietnamese legend, the king of the dragons, Lac Long Quan, married Au Co, a fairy of the bird kingdom. Together, they had 100 sons. Their firstborn was Hung Vuong, who became the ruler of the first Vietnamese dynasty. Because of this story, the Vietnamese call themselves the children of the dragon.

A BUSTLING CAPITAL

Hanoi is a big, bustling city with plenty to see, but what strikes Mia most is the traffic. The city's large streets are crammed with bicycles and cars, though most people are zipping along on motorbikes. There are traffic lights, but everyone seems to ignore them, aggressively moving forward even when the light is red.

The first time they cross a busy street, Mia is terrified. But Grandma points out locals who are walking into traffic without fear. She explains that if they walk slow and steady, the bikes and

THE ONE PILLAR PAGODA

One of Hanoi's most beloved landmarks is the One Pillar Pagoda. It was designed by Emperor Ly Thai Ton, who ruled Vietnam from 1028 to 1054. Legend holds that Quan The Am Bo Tat, the Goddess of Mercy, appeared to him in a dream. She handed a baby boy to the emperor, who at the time had no heir to the throne. Inspired by the dream, Ly Thai Ton married a young woman, who gave birth to a son. He had the One Pillar Pagoda built in gratitude to Quan The Am Bo Tat for helping fulfill his wish for an heir.

cars will find a way around them. Trying to look confident, Mia takes a breath and steps off the curb, with her mother and grandmother at each side. Grandma is right. The vehicles avoid them, and the family makes it safely to the other sidewalk.

They spend most of their time in Hanoi in the Old Quarter. Mia's mother is an architect. She is excited to look at all the different styles of buildings in the neighborhood.

Mia's mom marvels at how modern skyscrapers stand near French mansions built in the 1800s and religious temples from ancient times. That is not the only way the Old Quarter is an exciting mixture of the past and the present. Wandering through the streets of the Old Quarter, Mia watches stylishly dressed young people on motorbikes buzz by vendors wearing traditional conical straw hats as they push street carts and peddle their wares.

The neighborhood is a mosaic of colors, noises, and most of all, smells coming from the countless food stalls and shops that line the streets. The family usually eats breakfast at small cafés.

Students often come to the Temple of Literature to pray for good luck before taking exams.

Mia's mother and grandmother enjoy *ca phe trung*, black coffee flavored with sugar, condensed milk, and egg yolk. Amy tells Mia it is too strong and will keep her awake at night. But when Amy goes to the restroom, Grandma lets Mia have a few sips.

For most other meals, they eat street food while sitting on little plastic chairs outside a food stall. Grandma wants to try all sorts of rice and noodle dishes. To her surprise, Mia develops a taste for *mien luon xao*, noodles stir-fried with eel and black pepper, and *bun rieu cua*, a crab noodle soup topped with fish eggs.

SEEING THE SIGHTS

Grandma has a long list of places she wants to visit. They spend one afternoon touring the National Museum of Vietnamese History and another wandering through the galleries of the Vietnam National Fine Arts Museum. One morning, they go to Lake Hoan Kiem, where many people gather on the shores to practice tai chi, an ancient Chinese form of exercise. Crossing a bright red bridge, Grandma, Amy, and Mia reach a small island with a Taoist temple full of people praying and lighting incense.

At Grandma's insistence, they also stop at the Temple of Literature, one of the most popular attractions in Hanoi. The beautiful complex was built in 1070 to honor the Chinese philosopher Confucius, whose teachings many Vietnamese people still follow. Mia admires the beautiful gates, a pavilion, a lake, and ancient stones with writing engraved on their faces.

Mia's favorite attraction is the famous Thang Long Water Puppet Theater. At the theater, she watches a show featuring water puppetry, a unique Vietnamese theatrical tradition. Puppeteers hidden by a screen use long poles tied to wooden figures of people and animals to make the puppets walk and dance along a stage floor of water.

PALACES AND BEACHES

After three days in Hanoi, the family boards a plane. Within about 70 minutes, they arrive in the city of Hue in central Vietnam.[2] There they tour the Imperial City, a complex of palaces and other buildings constructed in the early 1800s, when Hue was the capital of the Vietnamese empire.

They admire the ornate thrones and lavish tombs of past emperors and stroll through the complex's extensive gardens.

Grandma insists they splurge on dinner at a fancy restaurant that serves *am thuc cung dinh Hue*. It is the type of cuisine that was served to the royal court. Their waiter explains that at each meal the king was served up to 50 dishes, including what were called the "eight treasures."[3] These special dishes used exotic ingredients, such as peacock meat and deer tendons. Am thuc cung dinh Hue cuisine was prepared with great ritual. Each dish had to be delicious, healthy, and look beautiful on the plate.

The metropolitan area of Ho Chi Minh City has a population of more than 9.3 million.[4]

After a few days in Hue, the travelers set out for Nha Trang. With its long coastline and warm weather, Vietnam is known for its beaches, and Nha Trang is one of its most famous beach resort areas. After days of sightseeing and travel, Mia is happy to have the chance to relax on the beach and take the occasional dip in the South China Sea. On their second day at the resort, they go for a boat ride to the islands just offshore. During the trip, Mia and her mother see coral reefs and angelfish as they snorkel in the crystal clear waters.

HO CHI MINH CITY

Feeling refreshed, the family begins the final leg of the journey with a flight to Ho Chi Minh City in southern Vietnam. It is the country's biggest city and just as bustling as Hanoi. Like the capital, it has chaotic roadways, a hectic street culture, and plenty of interesting things to do. They stay in an elegant European-style hotel built during the late 1800s when France controlled Vietnam as a colony. Nearby is Dong Khoi Street, the city's main shopping street. Mia buys souvenirs from traditional craftspeople, including a lacquerware bowl and an embroidered silk scarf.

Amy wants to visit various architectural landmarks, including the ornate Opera House and Notre Dame, a famous church known for its tall twin spires. Grandma suggests they go to Cho Lon, a neighborhood where many people of Chinese ethnicity live. There they climb to the fourth story of the Ten Thousand Buddhas Temple, where they see a 23-foot (7 m) statue of the religious figure Buddha wearing a gold robe and sitting on a lotus flower.[5]

One particularly hot afternoon, they walk through a pedestrian park at Bach Dang Wharf along the Saigon River. Mia cools down with a snack of coconut ice cream. She watches street performers singing and playing music in the park.

While in southern Vietnam, Grandma wants to take a side trip to the Mekong River delta, an area of rich farmland at the mouth of the Mekong, Vietnam's longest river. Traveling through the delta on a tour boat, Mia feels a world away from Ho Chi Minh City. The area is full of small villages where

RENAMING SAIGON

In the mid-1800s, Saigon became the capital of the French protectorate of Cochinchina, which was located in what is now southern Vietnam. It also served as the capital of South Vietnam after the country was divided in 1954. Following the Vietnam War (1954–1975), Saigon was renamed Ho Chi Minh City after the revolutionary leader who had helped win the war and reunite the nation. However, most residents still refer to their city by the old name of Saigon.

farmers, wearing traditional Vietnamese straw hats, grow rice in large paddies. It reminds Grandma of her childhood. She says she's pleased that not everything in Vietnam has changed.

CONFRONTING THE WAR

After they return to Ho Chi Minh City, Grandma announces that there is one more thing she wants to see: the War Remnants Museum. When Amy asks whether she's sure, Grandma nods firmly. The museum features exhibits about the horrors the Vietnamese people suffered during the Vietnam War (1954–1975), which Vietnamese people call the American War. Mia can barely look at many of the photographs displayed, which show the bodies of Vietnamese civilians killed by US troops and people horribly burned by chemicals from US bombs.

When the war began, Vietnam was divided into two countries—North Vietnam and South Vietnam. North Vietnam had a Communist government. South Vietnam was a republic led by a dictator. North Vietnam took up arms to unify the country, which many people in the south, aided by US troops, fought to stop. North Vietnam won the war and brought all of Vietnam under Communist rule.

Mia remembered that Grandpa had worked as a translator for the US Army. When the Communists took over South Vietnam, he was afraid he would be arrested and jailed. He and Grandma escaped to the United States. After being sent to a refugee camp in Oklahoma, they moved to California, determined to begin their lives anew. Two years later, their daughter was born. They gave her the American name Amy as a way of embracing their new homeland.

After they leave the museum, Mia and her family go to a nearby café. No one speaks. They are all overwhelmed by what they have seen. Grandma starts to cry quietly. Amy says they never should have gone to the museum, but Grandma insists she is glad they did. She explains that when she first left Vietnam, it was a devastated country, torn apart by decades of war. Grandma was sure she would never be able to return.

But now here she is, with her daughter and granddaughter, introducing them to Vietnam as a thriving, modern nation. Looking at Mia, Grandma explains she's not upset. She is crying with the joy that she is finally able to share her country with those she loves most.

OLD AND NEW

Vietnam offers many exciting, unique experiences to visitors and residents alike.

The War Remnants Museum includes an exhibit about the harm a chemical called Agent Orange caused during the war.

People can enjoy nature, see beautiful islands, and visit a floating village at Ha Long Bay.

Its largest cities, Hanoi and Ho Chi Minh City, showcase a vibrant, modern culture coexisting with ancient landmarks that hint at the country's rich history. Its rural areas present comparatively tranquil settings where many Vietnamese villagers live in much the same way their ancestors did. Its mountainous region features beautiful scenery, while its coast boasts spectacular beaches.

However, everywhere in modern Vietnam holds evidence of the country's troubled past. Throughout much of its history, Vietnam has had its independence threatened by other nations. The resiliency of the Vietnamese people has allowed them to repeatedly repel foreign invaders. Yet through contact with foreigners, they have also absorbed many cultural influences. As a result, modern Vietnamese culture is infused with foreign elements such as Chinese religion, French architecture, and American popular music while retaining its own unique and fascinating character.

CHAPTER **TWO**

GEOGRAPHY

Located in Southeast Asia, Vietnam lies on the eastern edge of the Indochinese Peninsula. The country shares borders with China to the north. Laos and Cambodia are to the west.

Vietnam's coastline is 2,140 miles (3,444 km) long and runs along three bodies of water: the Gulf of Tonkin to the northeast, the South China Sea to the east and south, and the Gulf of Thailand to the southwest. With a total area of 127,881 square miles (331,210 sq km), Vietnam is about the same size as Norway and a little bigger than the US state of New Mexico.[1]

On a map, Vietnam appears as a long, slender country. From north to south, Vietnam runs 1,025 miles (1,650 km), and at its narrowest point in the nation's central region, it measures only about 31 miles (50 km) wide.[2] Its shape, which is broad in the north,

Nha Trang has a 3.7-mile (6 km) sandy beach for visitors to enjoy.

narrow in the center, and broad again in the south, has been said to resemble the letter S or a dragon.

THREE REGIONS

Low mountains and hills are found in about three-fourths of Vietnam's land. The other quarter features tropical lowlands.[3] The Vietnamese generally think of the country as three separate regions: the north, the center, and the south.

In the north is the Red River delta, a flat, triangular area. The Red River is the country's second-longest river. Its tributaries bring water to this fertile and densely populated region, which is home to the Vietnamese capital of Hanoi.[4]

Only a few feet above sea level, this low area often floods during seasonal rains, although for centuries the Vietnamese have used a network of dikes and canals to control and make use of the river's flow. To its north and the northwest, the Red River delta is ringed by the Annamese Cordillera mountain range, also known as Truong Son. The most inaccessible region of the country, these northern highlands include Vietnam's highest mountains.

THE ISLANDS OF HA LONG BAY

Off the northeastern coast of Vietnam, Ha Long Bay in the Gulf of Tonkin features more than 1,600 small pillar-like limestone islands covered with lush green forests.[5] The bay's name, which means "descending dragon," refers to an ancient legend of a mother dragon who defeated her enemies by raining fire and emeralds upon them. The emeralds then turned into the bay's unique islands, which have become a major tourist attraction.

MAP OF VIETNAM

KEY:

- Capital
- City
- Point of Interest

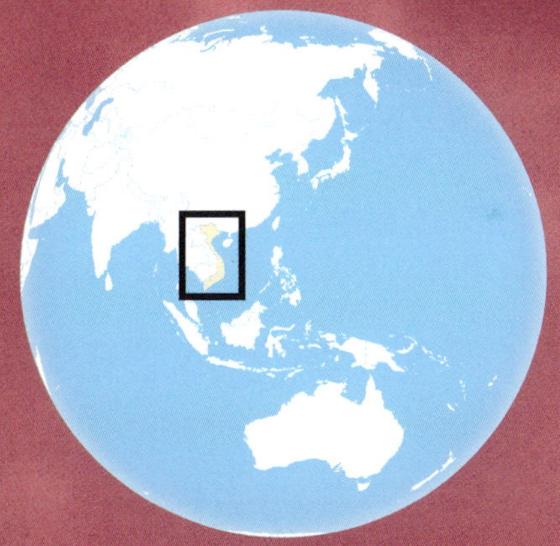

The highest point in Vietnam is Fan Si Peak, which stands 10,315 feet (3,144 m) high.[8]

The central region of Vietnam includes a long, narrow strip of coastland along the shore of the South China Sea. On the western side of this strip, the Annamese Cordillera range towers over these lowlands, which include the coastal cities of Hue, Hoi An, and Da Nang. The Annamese Cordillera continues south into the central highlands. This plateau area, dotted with rugged peaks toward the west, covers 51,800 square miles (134,160 sq km).[6]

Southern Vietnam is dominated by the vast Mekong River delta. This low-level plain is a web of rivers and canals. It includes much of the country's best agricultural land, earning it the nickname of Vietnam's Rice Bowl. The Mekong, Vietnam's longest river, is easily navigable and plays an important role in the country's shipping industry. To the north of the Mekong delta, Ho Chi Minh City serves as the nation's most important economic hub.

CLIMATE AND SEASONS

Vietnam's climate is mainly hot, with substantial rainfall throughout the year. The average daily humidity is 84 percent, making for many warm, sticky days.[7] But some variations in temperature and rainfall do exist between the northern and southern regions. Altitude also affects the climate, with variations found between coastal areas and highlands.

Vietnam has two seasons, although the seasonal differences tend to be more dramatic in the north than in the south. During summer, which lasts from roughly May to October, monsoon winds bring heated air from the southwest, causing hot temperatures and heavy rains. The winter, from roughly November through April, is considered the dry season, although monsoons from the northeast also bring some precipitation during these months. About 10 percent of yearly rainfall occurs during the winter dry season.[9]

Annual rainfall is high everywhere in Vietnam, but the amount varies by location. Hanoi in the north receives about 68 inches (173 cm) of rain each year, while the lowlands in the south see about 80 inches (203 cm). The mountains, which are the wettest part of the country, can have yearly rainfalls of more than 160 inches (406 cm).[10]

Severe rainfalls frequently occur from May through January during typhoon season. Typhoons are the same type of storm as hurricanes, but they form in the northwestern Pacific Ocean. Typhoons can cause flooding, which is often worst in the deltas, but these storms usually do the most damage along the central coast. The wind and rain produced by typhoons can cause extensive property damage and even deaths. For instance, landslides and rising river levels triggered by Super Typhoon Yagi killed at least 143 people in the Red River region in 2024.[11]

THE WORLD'S LARGEST CAVE SYSTEM

In 2009, a British team became the first people known to explore Son Doong, a complex of hundreds of caves in Phong Nha–Ke Bang National Park in the Annamese Cordillera range. Most of the caves are connected, forming the largest cave system in the world. It measures about 1.36 billion cubic feet (38.5 million cubic m).[12] The cave system includes a jungle and a large underground river. It also has its own weather system, which often produces clouds within the caves.

Super Typhoon Yagi caused major flooding in Hanoi. It was the strongest storm Vietnam had experienced in 70 years.

The north is the coolest part of Vietnam. Generally, high temperatures range from 60 degrees Fahrenheit (16°C) in the winter to 90 degrees Fahrenheit (32°C) in the summer.[13] In the mountains of the far north, temperatures are often lower, sometimes even falling below the freezing point. Snow can often be seen on Fan Si Peak.

Because of its high altitude, the plateau of the central highlands experiences moderate temperatures, with highs generally between 64 and 77 degrees Fahrenheit (18 and 25°C).[14] The southern and the central coasts are warmer, with high temperatures ranging from 70 to 90 degrees Fahrenheit (21–32°C).[15] However, breezes off the water can make the coastal region feel cooler, even in the summer.

ENVIRONMENTAL ISSUES

Vietnam faces a variety of environmental threats, largely stemming from decades of rapid population growth and industrialization, coupled with inadequate land management and government regulation. The destruction of forests by the agriculture and timber industries has led to deforestation and soil erosion. Farmlands have been damaged by excessive use of pesticides and fertilizers. Many waterways are highly polluted, as is the air in most urban centers.

The construction of hydroelectric plants in the central highlands that divert natural water sources, coupled with inadequate waste treatment, have left many communities without safe drinking water.

Vietnamese people have increasingly voiced concerns about the country's environmental struggles. In the early 2010s, a Chinese-backed bauxite mining project in the central highlands drew growing criticism from scientists and environmentalists. They feared the operation would contaminate nearby water and soil with chemicals. A massive chemical spill along Vietnam's central coast in 2016 caused outrage from environmental experts and ordinary citizens alike. The government's limited response to this environmental disaster, one of the worst in Vietnam's history, was met with large protests that authorities ended with mass arrests.

The government has increasingly sought to punish environmentalists, particularly climate change activists. The government considers the activists' concerns an intolerable attack on one-party Communist rule. Government officials punish environmental activist groups by repeatedly jailing their leaders, usually on false charges of

THE SPRATLY ISLANDS

The Spratly Islands in the South China Sea have long been disputed territory. Several countries, including Vietnam and China, claim this island group, which is a prime fishing area surrounded by rich undersea oil reserves. The islands have been the site of frequent clashes between the Vietnamese and Chinese navies. In the early 2020s, Vietnam began dredging soil to increase the size of the islands where it has military outposts. The island-building project allows Vietnam to send more ships and soldiers to defend its claims on the Spratlys.

In addition to other pollution concerns, Vietnam struggles with air pollution. Construction and areas packed with motorists cause smog, making Hanoi one of the most air-polluted cities in the world.

tax evasion. But as the recent environmental movement in Vietnam and international anger over the arrests grow, the country will likely find it difficult to silence all the voices speaking against its environmental policy.

CHAPTER **THREE**

PLANTS AND ANIMALS

In spring 1992, a group of biologists traveled to a remote area in western Vietnam. During their research expedition, they entered a village to buy food. In a hunter's hut, they found something they had never expected to see: a pair of long horns that were unrecognizable to them.

This encounter led to the scientific discovery of the saola—a species of animal previously unknown to the scientific world. This forest-dwelling oxlike creature is distinguished by its chocolate-colored coat, white markings on its face and throat, and its spindle-like black horns about two times the length of its head.[1]

However, the saola was not the only new life-form found in Vietnam. In recent decades, hundreds

Vietnam is home to almost 10 percent of all known species of animals.

Not closely related to any other known animal, the saola was the largest land-dwelling mammal to be discovered since 1937. There are still very few photos of the animal.

of previously unknown plants and animals have been discovered there. These findings are a testament to Vietnam's extreme biological diversity. In terms of area, Vietnam is the sixty-seventh largest nation.[2] Yet it ranks as the sixteenth-most biodiverse country in the world.[3]

FORESTS AND VEGETATION

Much of Vietnam is covered with trees or other forms of plant life. Forests make up about 45 percent of its area, while another 35 percent is devoted to farmland and pastures.[4] Many unforested and uncultivated lands are havens for bamboo, brushwood, weeds, and tall grass.

Vietnam has more than 13,000 species of plants and more than 10,000 species of animals.[5]

Vietnam's mountainous regions are home to thick forests of deciduous trees and evergreens. Common trees found there include pine, ebony, and teak. These hardwoods are important to the country's lumber industry because of their use in furniture. Many mountain forests are also dense with woody vines and broad-leaved plants.

The rich soil of the Mekong delta makes it lush with greenery. Its marshlands contain forests of mangroves, whose roots often arch above the water, providing a comfortable habitat for many fish, reptiles, and birds. The delta's tropical forests also include many types of fruit trees, such as mango, banana, and papaya.

Coconut palms are found throughout much of Vietnam but are especially prevalent in the Mekong River delta and the central coast. Their fruit and oil are common ingredients in

Vietnamese cooking. Their wood is used for building boats. Their large, strong leaves provide materials for thatched roofs on rural houses, as well as fiber for mats and other traditional crafts.

Throughout Vietnam, flowering plants add color to the landscape. The paulownia, a tree native to Vietnam and southern China, brightens spring with its purple blossoms. The slopes of the Annamese Cordillera mountains take on a pink hue when wild rhododendron plants bloom. Orchids also grow wild, particularly in the Mekong delta. Both wild and cultivated varieties of this popular flower are exported to countries around the world. The lotus, the national flower of Vietnam, is common on the surfaces of ponds and lakes. This flower symbolizes beauty overcoming darkness in Vietnamese culture.

AGENT ORANGE

During the Vietnam War, US military aircraft sprayed the forests of central Vietnam with a mix of herbicides called Agent Orange to destroy foliage in which Vietnamese fighters could hide from US troops. Agent Orange killed wide swaths of the country's forests and contaminated its water supply. Many Vietnamese have blamed a rise in human miscarriages, birth defects, and cancers on their exposure to these harmful chemicals.

ANIMALS OF VIETNAM

Vietnam's forests contain many types of large mammals, including wild oxen, wild boar, and deer. Some of the large animals most closely associated with the country, however, are now close to extinction. For instance, the clouded leopard, the Asian elephant, and the Asiatic black bear are now rarely seen in the wild.

Various parts of the lotus plant are used as ingredients in traditional Vietnamese dishes and medicines.

Common smaller mammals include porcupines, hares, otters, mongooses, skunks, and squirrels. The country also boasts more than two dozen species of primates, including gibbons, macaques, lorises, and langurs.[6] Animals raised on farms include pigs, goats, ducks, chickens, and cattle.

About 850 species of birds live in Vietnam.[7] The swamps of the Mekong River delta are a particularly inviting habitat for both native and migratory birds. Among the birds in the region are the red-headed crane, white-breasted kingfisher, and green bee-eater. The slopes of the Annamese Cordillera mountains provide a home for the Annamese silver pheasant, easily spotted by its red legs and face and silvery feathers.

Vietnam's waterways teem with reptiles, including lizards, pythons, and cobras. Crocodiles are found in the wild in some lakes, but they are also commercially raised for their meat. Among the many insects of Vietnam are mosquitoes, centipedes, dragonflies, and ants. Butterflies such as the white dragontail, red lacewing, and jungle queen are also common, with 440 species found in Cat Tien National Park in southern Vietnam.[8]

THE WATER BUFFALO

The domesticated water buffalo has long been revered in Vietnamese culture. Many traditional farmers still rely on these working animals to plow their fields. Children often have the responsibility of taking care of a farming family's water buffalo. This is an important task, as the animal is often a farmer's most valuable possession. Because of its economic importance to Vietnamese culture, the water buffalo is seen as a symbol of prosperity and well-being.

In 2014, the second-largest insect in the world was found in Vietnam. The stick insect, known to entomologists as *Phryganistria heusii yentuensis,* measures 21 inches (53 cm) long with its legs extended.[9]

Many freshwater fish are found in Vietnam. About 1,200 species live in the Mekong River alone, making the river the world's largest inland fishery.[10] Vietnam's long shoreline also makes it inviting to a wide variety of corals. Coral reefs along offshore islands in turn create a habitat for many types of fish, mollusks, turtles, and eels. Dugongs, also called sea cows, feed off seagrass near reefs. Other marine mammals found along the coast include dolphins, porpoises, and whales.

***Vagrans egista sinha*, commonly known as the Himalayan vagrant butterfly, is one of many butterfly species found in Vietnam.**

THREATS TO WILDLIFE

Tigers used to roam the countryside of northern Vietnam. Today, these mighty creatures are all but extinct in the country. Scientists estimate that fewer than 50 tigers are left, but none have been photographed in the wild since 1998.[11] Vietnam's list of other endangered animals includes the white-rumped black lemur, river terrapin, spoon-billed sandpiper, Siamese crocodile, and Indochinese box turtle. Even the recently discovered saola may not survive for long.

Many factors are to blame for animal species dying out in Vietnam. As the country's population has grown, human settlement and infrastructure have encroached on previously wild spaces. Clearing forests for logging, agriculture, and other human activities has destroyed many natural habitats. Pollution of the water and the air also threaten the health of many animal species.

But perhaps the greatest threat to animals in Vietnam is poaching. While snaring and trapping protected wildlife is illegal, many hunters defy the law for financial gain. Some animals have been hunted to near extinction because certain body parts can bring high prices on the black market. For instance, rhinoceroses have been hunted for their horns, which are considered status items. Bears are killed to extract their bile, which is used in medicines by traditional healers.

Many animals are killed for their meat, which is often served to wealthy patrons at high-end restaurants. The pangolin is an armadillo-like animal that is the most common victim of wildlife trafficking. Its meat can sell for the equivalent of $500 per pound (0.5 kg).[12]

To help preserve its wildlife, the Vietnamese government has established 30 national parks.[13] The largest, Yok Don National Park, houses 67 species of animals, 38 of which are considered endangered.[14] Hunting park animals is against the law, but law enforcement is generally lax. Poachers often bribe park rangers and set snares and traps without fear of getting caught.

Vietnam's government has established several rescue centers for wild animals seized from wildlife traffickers. The animals are restored to health and bred if possible. The healthiest are sometimes returned to the wild, although many are incapable of living outside of captivity. In 2020, the Vietnamese government issued a directive aimed at strengthening enforcement of existing wildlife protection laws. Conservationists welcome such measures, but they insist that the Vietnamese public and government must do more if the country's most threatened wildlife is to survive.

FIGHTING WILDLIFE TRAFFICKING

In Vietnam, many well-intentioned park rangers do not have any experience in combating wildlife trafficking. The conservation organization WildAct is working to change that. Founded by wildlife conservation scientist Trang Nguyen in 2015, it provides training to rangers and volunteers in removing animal snares from parks and giving first aid to injured animals. WildAct is just one of many organizations encouraging the Vietnamese public, especially its young people, to protect the country's most threatened animal life.

CHAPTER **FOUR**

HISTORY

Although it is uncertain when prehistoric people first lived in Vietnam, archaeological sites in the province of Thanh Hoa suggest humans lived there about 500,000 years ago. About 5,000 years ago, Viet people, today the largest ethnic group in Vietnam, were farming in the Red River delta. They were ruled by the Hung dynasty kings of Van Lang, the first state formed in present-day Vietnam.

From about 800 to 300 BCE, the Dong Son civilization developed in the delta. Its people used dikes and canals to irrigate rice fields and made tools and weapons from bronze. The best-known artifacts of the Dong Son people are large, decorated bronze drums, which were likely played during ceremonies and rituals.

In 258 BCE, the Hung king was overthrown by An Duong, who united the land of the Dong Son people

My Son Sanctuary was built between the 300s and 1200s CE under the Champa Kingdom. Its towers served as Hindu temples.

with his highland kingdom to form Au Lac. The Au Lac kingdom lasted only until 207 BCE. That year, Trieu Da, an official with the Qin dynasty that ruled China, took control of Au Lac, which along with other kingdoms to the north became the independent Nam Viet. China's Han emperors added Nam Viet to China's territory in 111 BCE. China controlled the region for the next 1,000 years.

During this period, many aspects of Chinese culture were introduced to the people of Nam Viet. These included ideas about government, philosophy, education, architecture, language, and literature. Particularly influential were the belief systems now known as the three teachings in Vietnam: Buddhism, Confucianism, and Taoism.

THE TRUNG SISTERS

In 39 CE, a Viet widow named Trung Trac decided to take over her husband's plot against Chinese authorities after he was assassinated. She recruited her younger sister, Trung Nhi, and together they led an army against the Chinese. After taking over many military fortresses, they declared themselves queens of a new independent nation. Lacking sufficient arms and training, their army was eventually defeated by Chinese troops. The Trung sisters then drowned themselves in the Red River where it met the Day River. A street in Ho Chi Minh City bears the name of these courageous warriors, who are now considered national heroines.

Based on the instruction of the ancient religious figure known as the Buddha, Buddhism aims to free its followers from suffering. Confucianism, promoted by the Chinese philosopher Confucius, is concerned with morality and social order. Taoism is an ancient Chinese philosophy that stresses living in balance and harmony with the universe. The ideas associated with these three belief systems were much more readily adopted by the ruling class than by average people.

AN INDEPENDENT KINGDOM

The Viet often resisted Chinese rule, but it was not until 939 CE that they were able to stage a successful rebellion. Taking advantage of political turmoil in China, revolutionary leader Ngo Quyen defeated the Chinese, although he continued to pay tribute to their emperor. After Ngo Quyen's death in 944, the region fell into chaos as warlords battled for control.

What became known as Dai Viet finally stabilized under the leadership of two Vietnamese dynasties. These were the Ly dynasty, which began in 1009, followed by the Tran dynasty, which began in 1225. The Vietnamese kings of these dynasties modeled their courts after those of Chinese emperors, while villagers continued to maintain their own customs and beliefs.

In 1400, Ho Quy Ly took the throne and became the emperor of the short-lived

Ngo Quyen's rule faced resistance from many regional lords, but he maintained control over the area.

Gia Long ruled as emperor from 1802 to 1820. His reign saw the establishment of a postal service and of grain storage so there was food in times of famine.

Ho dynasty. Only seven years later, China, now under the Ming dynasty, invaded the kingdom and once again took control over present-day northern Vietnam. Rebel leader Le Loi gathered enough support to drive out the Chinese in 1428 during the Lam Son Uprising. Now a national hero in Vietnam, Le Loi established himself as the emperor of the Le dynasty.

During the Le dynasty, Dai Viet expanded into the south to acquire new farmland. By the late 1400s, its emperors had taken over the Champa kingdom in what is now central Vietnam. In the late 1600s, they moved farther south, eventually gaining dominance over the Mekong River delta. Despite its successes in territorial expansion, the Le dynasty experienced many periods of political unrest. By the mid-1500s, two families within the Le court were battling each other for control. In 1600, the country became divided, with the Trinh family ruling the north and the Nguyen family ruling the south.

A peasant rebellion in the late 1700s upended the rule of both families and led to the end of the Le dynasty. Nguyen Phuc Anh raised an army and reunited the country in 1802. Ruling under the name Gia Long, the emperor of the new Nguyen dynasty named his kingdom Vietnam and established its capital at the city of Hue on the central coast.

THE FRENCH IN VIETNAM

Since the early 1600s, French priests had been present in Vietnam, where they sought to convert the local population to Roman Catholicism. When the Nguyen dynasty opposed their efforts, the Catholic missionaries persuaded the French government to take action. In the 1850s, France sent

French influence can still be seen in the architecture of Vietnam. Construction on St. Joseph's Cathedral in Hanoi began in 1886.

warships to Vietnam. France claimed it was to protect French priests and their converts, but the actual plan was to take control of the country so France could use Vietnam as a base to increase its trade with China. By the end of the 1800s, France had colonized Vietnam and its neighbors Cambodia and Laos, which were known collectively as Indochina.

The French built roads and railroads, improved Vietnam's ports, and established plantations that grew coffee, tea, and rubber plants. But many Vietnamese resented French rule after they had maintained a hard-won independence for 900 years. Seeking to free themselves, they formed political parties and organizations promoting revolution. Among them was the Indochinese Communist Party, which was founded by Ho Chi Minh in 1930.

During World War II (1939–1945), the French government surrendered to Germany, which along with Japan and Italy made up the Axis powers. These nations opposed the Allies, which were led by the United Kingdom, the United States, and the Union of Soviet Socialist Republics (USSR). In 1940, the Japanese government forced France to allow its military to occupy Indochina.

At first, aspiring Vietnamese revolutionaries believed that the Japanese might help free them from the French. However, they quickly recognized the Japanese presence as another threat to their independence. Ho and other Communist leaders formed the Viet Minh organization in 1941 as part of their continuing resistance movement.

On August 14, 1945, Japan surrendered, marking the Axis powers' total defeat in World War II. Days later, the Viet Minh staged an uprising called the August Revolution. On September 2, Ho announced the creation of the independent country of the Democratic Republic of Vietnam (DRV). But France did not want to relinquish control of Vietnam. After several military clashes, France and the DRV went to war at the end of 1946. After eight years of fighting, the Viet Minh forces conquered the French military base at Dien Bien Phu, leading to France's defeat in 1954.

THE VIETNAM WAR

Peace talks held in Geneva, Switzerland, led to a series of agreements called the Geneva Accords in 1954. They temporarily split Vietnam in two along the seventeenth parallel line of latitude, creating the Democratic Republic of Vietnam in the north and the Republic of Vietnam in the south. The accords stipulated that an election would soon be held to bring the entire nation under unified rule. But many Vietnamese in the south did not want an election. They feared Ho

After Vietnam was divided in 1954, about 820,000 Vietnamese, mostly Catholics, moved from North to South Vietnam.[2]

would win and bring the entire country under Communist rule.

The United States, which had supported French rule in southern Vietnam, held the same fear. At the time, the United States' primary enemy was the USSR, a large Communist nation in northern Asia and eastern Europe. The USSR included Russia and a number of smaller republics. The United States did not want Communism to spread and the USSR's influence on the world to grow. The US State Department believed that if Vietnam turned Communist, other countries in Southeast Asia would follow.

In 1955, fighting broke out between North and South Vietnam. Revolutionaries in the south tried to remove the US-backed anti-Communist government headed by Ngo Dinh Diem. Often called the Second Indochina War, the conflict became known in the United States as the Vietnam War and in Vietnam as the American War. The United States at first sent advisers, funding, and military equipment to help the southern forces defeat the Communists. As the war escalated, it began sending military troops. By 1967, there were 500,000 US soldiers in Vietnam.[1]

South Vietnam appeared to be winning until January 30, 1968, when the North Vietnamese army and guerrillas from the Viet Cong military organization staged the Tet Offensive. This massive attack coincided with Vietnam's New Year's celebration. The Tet Offensive did not topple the South Vietnamese government, but it signaled that North Vietnam might be able to win the war. Meanwhile, many Americans had turned against US involvement in Vietnam. Massive protests

MINI **BIO**

HO CHI MINH

The revolutionary leader Ho Chi Minh devoted his life to freeing Vietnam from French and US control and establishing it as an independent Communist nation. Born Nguyen Sinh Cung in 1890, Ho embraced Communism while living in France as a young man. In 1930, Ho founded the Indochinese Communist Party in Vietnam. Facing the death sentence under French rule if he returned to Vietnam, he continued to promote revolution while in exile in other countries. He secretly returned to Vietnam in 1940 when it came under Japanese control. He then adopted the name Ho Chi Minh, meaning "he who enlightens."

After Japan was defeated in World War II, Ho declared Vietnam an independent nation on September 2, 1945, and became its president. France refused to recognize its independence, leading to the First Indochina War in late 1946. Ho's Viet Minh forces took control of the countryside by 1953 and defeated the French army the following year. In the peace treaty, Vietnam was divided, with Ho in charge of North Vietnam.

Ho secured financial aid for North Vietnam from the USSR and China as war broke out between North Vietnam and the US-supported South Vietnam. In 1969, Ho died just as negotiations for ending the Vietnam War were beginning. Six years after his death, his dream of a reunified Vietnam under Communist rule was finally realized.

Ho Chi Minh was born on May 19, 1890.

By the end of the Vietnam War, more than a million Vietnamese troops had fought for South Vietnam.

THE SON MY MEMORIAL

In the village of Son My in central Vietnam stands a memorial with 504 names inscribed on a wall.[5] It honors the victims of the massacre at My Lai, the US name for the village. On March 16, 1968, US soldiers helicoptered into My Lai and murdered most people there, including children as young as one year old. For 18 months, the United States covered up the massacre. When reports of what happened at My Lai finally surfaced, they turned many Americans against US involvement in the Vietnam War.

helped convince President Richard Nixon to withdraw US troops from the country in early 1973.

The fighting continued until April 1975, when the North Vietnamese army overran South Vietnam and captured its capital of Saigon, which was renamed Ho Chi Minh City. A year later, national elections were held. In July 1976, the country was formally reunified as the Socialist Republic of Vietnam.

The war left the nation in ruins. About three million Vietnamese soldiers and civilians died during the conflict.[3] Millions more became homeless. Most of Vietnam's industrial capacity, particularly in the north, was destroyed by US bombing campaigns.

AFTER THE WAR

Soon after the war, about 150,000 Vietnamese in the south fled the country.[4] Many of them eventually settled in the United States, Canada, or Australia. Some people who had supported the South Vietnamese government were unable to escape. They were jailed or sent to re-education camps by the Communist government. In these camps, prisoners were taught Communist ideas, forced to confess to crimes, and forced to perform hard labor.

Large-scale legal and illegal emigration continued for two decades. One of the largest waves came in 1978, when many Vietnamese people left the country by boat. Some drowned or were killed by pirates. By 1995, about 1.6 million Vietnamese had left their country as refugees.[6]

Many Vietnamese who remained in the country had their lives upended by the new government's massive resettlement program. This program aimed to relocate millions of people living in the Red River and Mekong River deltas to less populated areas in the highlands and mountains. Eventually, about 3.6 million people were resettled, many against their will.[7]

The government also set about transforming the Vietnamese economy. Following Communist ideals, officials began eliminating almost all privately owned businesses. The government nationalized most industries so that factories were owned and run by the state.

Economic productivity dropped as industries were plagued by waste, inefficiency, and poor quality control. The economy further suffered as the government poured money into military campaigns against Cambodia and China during the late 1970s. Increasingly, Vietnam had to rely on foreign aid, mostly from the USSR.

With the economy in shambles, the Vietnamese government was forced to change course. In 1986, it adopted a new policy called *doi moi*, meaning "renovation." Much to the amazement of conservative Communist politicians, it called for reforms that would make Vietnam's economy function more like those of capitalist nations such as the United States. Many businesses were privatized, exports were increased, and Vietnam began to seek new trade agreements with foreign countries. These measures became more important after 1989, when the USSR began to collapse.

The United Nations High Commission for Refugees worked with the new Vietnamese government to establish the Orderly Departure Program in 1975. As a result, people fleeing Vietnam could leave the country safely and legally rather than in small boats that were unsafe for sea travel.

With the end of the USSR in 1991, Vietnam lost not only the Soviet aid that propped up its economy but also its most important trading partner.

INTERNATIONAL RELATIONS

Vietnamese leaders knew they had to improve relations with the US government. In 1992, Vietnam announced that all officials of South Vietnam had been released from re-education camps. Two years later, President Bill Clinton lifted the US embargo on trade with Vietnam. An embargo is a ban on trade. Removing the embargo allowed US companies to do business with Vietnam for the first time since the end of the Vietnam War.

In 1995, Vietnam saw two more important changes. These were the restoration of diplomatic relations with the United States and admittance to the Association of Southeast Asian Nations. Membership in this regional organization helped Vietnam make trade deals with China, Singapore, Japan, and other countries in Asia.

In the early 2000s, Vietnam continued to adopt reforms aimed at improving its relations with other nations, strengthening trade ties, and attracting

BAMBOO DIPLOMACY

In 2021, Nguyen Phu Trong compared his country's foreign policy to the bamboo plant. Both had "strong roots, stout trunk, and flexible branches." Trong sought to keep Vietnam strong by being flexible in the way it dealt with foreign countries, with the goal of making "more friends, fewer foes."[8] He was especially concerned with maintaining good relations with both the United States and China, even as the tensions grew between these two superpowers in the early 2000s.

foreign investment. In 2001, it negotiated a new trade agreement with the United States, which made the United States the prime market for Vietnamese exports. Vietnam also joined the World Trade Organization in 2007 and the Trans-Pacific Partnership in 2016.

Nguyen Phu Trong is credited as the official most responsible for guiding Vietnam's recent economic transformation and international relations. Elected general secretary of Vietnam's Communist Party in 2011, he was the most powerful official in the government during the 13 years he held the post. He was a conservative politician, and he was admired for his practical problem-solving skills, especially in balancing the demands of superpowers such as the United States and China.

In 2015, Trong made history by being the first chief of Vietnam's Communist Party to travel to Washington, DC, and meet with a US president. Considered the most influential Vietnamese leader since the Vietnam War, his death in July 2024 led many people in Vietnam and abroad to speculate on the future of the country. People wondered whether the revitalization of Vietnam's economy and the country's rise on the world stage would continue as it did under Trong's watch.

CHAPTER **FIVE**

PEOPLE AND CULTURE

About 106 million people live in Vietnam, making it the sixteenth-most-populous country.[1] Vietnam is also one of the most densely populated nations in the world. As a comparison, Vietnam's population is about one-third of that of the United States.[2] However, Vietnam is only about one-thirtieth the United States' size.[3]

About 69 percent of Vietnamese people are between the ages of 15 and 65. The median age is 33 years, but that number is inching upward as life expectancy, now at 76, increases and the fertility rate decreases. On average, Vietnamese women have two children, with rural women likely to have more and urban women likely to have fewer.[4]

Luong Nhu Hoc Lantern Street is a popular place to visit after dark, when lanterns light the street lined with vendors selling lanterns and a variety of foods.

Vietnam's ethnic minorities, including Hmong people, celebrate their cultures in many ways, such as through traditional clothing and dance.

Vietnam's population remains largely rural, with only about 40 percent of its people living in cities.[5] However, the urban population is growing as young people move to cities in search of employment. Vietnam's largest urban area is Ho Chi Minh City, followed by Hanoi, Can Tho, Haiphong, Da Nang, and Bien Hoa.

ETHNICITY AND LANGUAGE

About 85 percent of Vietnamese belong to the Kinh, or Viet, ethnic group.[6] More than 50 ethnicities are represented in the remaining 15 percent of the population.[7] Many small ethnic groups with their own cultures and languages live in the country's mountains and highlands. Individuals from these groups also live in Vietnam's cities.

About 23 percent of people in Vietnam are 14 or younger. Just 8 percent are older than 64.[9]

Among the largest minority ethnic groups are the Tay and the Tai. The Tay are located to the north and northeast of the Red River delta, and the Tai live in the valley of the Red and Black Rivers in the northwest and north-central interior. Each group makes up approximately 1.9 percent of Vietnam's population.[8]

Other significant ethnic minorities include the Cham and the Khmer. The Cham are descendants of the original inhabitants of the central coast. The Khmer, related to the people of Cambodia, are found mostly along the Vietnamese border with that country and near the mouth of the Mekong River. The Hoa, an ethnically Chinese minority, live mainly in cities. Historically, they played an important role in Vietnam's commerce and trade.

During the thousand-year period when China controlled Vietnam, Chinese was the language of the royal court. But Vietnamese survived as the language spoken by commoners. However, many of the words used in modern Vietnamese are of Chinese origin. Vietnamese has incorporated many French and English words as well.

Vietnamese is the official language of the country. But people in minority ethnic groups primarily speak their own language in daily life, even if they know and use Vietnamese as a second language. In urban areas, English is widely taught in schools and is the most commonly heard foreign language. Other languages spoken in Vietnam include Chinese, French, and Russian.

TRADITIONAL CRAFTS AND MODERN ART

Throughout their history, Vietnamese people have crafted beautiful objects. One of their most famous traditional arts is lacquerware. Craftspeople decorate wooden objects with pearls, shells, and pieces of silver and gold. They then coat them with many layers of tree sap until the surface takes on a glossy sheen.

Vietnamese people are also known for their ceramic making, an art they learned from the

WRITING THE VIETNAMESE LANGUAGE

For centuries, the written form of the Vietnamese language used Chinese characters. But in the 1600s, Roman Catholic missionaries, hoping to minimize Chinese influence over Vietnamese culture, developed a writing system with the Roman alphabet. This alphabet is used in English and many other European languages. When the French took control of Vietnam in the late 1800s, this writing system became the standard. As a result, Vietnam is one of the few Southeast Asian countries that uses romanized script for written communication.

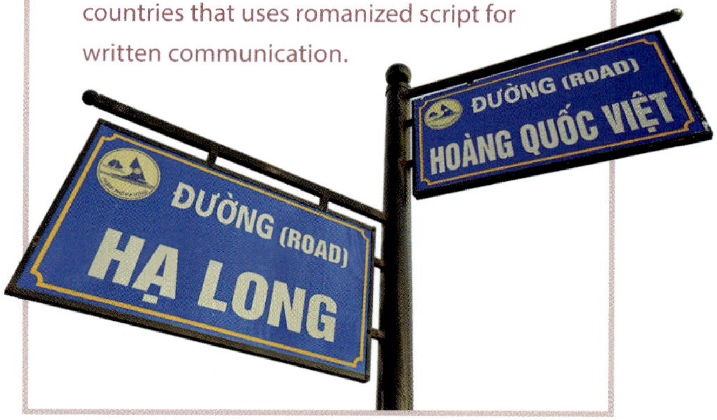

Lacquer was traditionally made from sap from lacquer trees. The exact recipes that artists used were kept secret.

Chinese, and for block printing. In this printing technique, a craftsperson carves an image into a block of wood, inks its surface, and presses the block onto a sheet of paper. In an old painting style called Hang Trong, artists use block printing to create a black-and-white lined image and then fill in the spaces with brilliant colors.

In 1925, French officials opened the School of Fine Arts of Indochina in Hanoi. Instructors there introduced Vietnamese artists to the European tradition of painting canvases with oil paint. For many decades, classical French painting styles dominated Vietnamese visual arts.

While the government supported the revival of traditional arts, it did nothing to promote more modern forms. Only in the 1990s did contemporary artists begin to receive training in modern techniques and subjects and begin to display their work in galleries. During this time, five graduates from the University of Fine Arts in Hanoi were nicknamed the Gang of Five and received international acclaim for their bold and emotional abstract works.

MUSIC, THEATER, AND LITERATURE

Much of Vietnam's musical tradition has roots in performances given before the imperial court. They featured costumed dancers and musicians playing instruments such as the zither, lute, and bamboo xylophone. Popular court music styles included *nha nhac*, which featured a prominent drumbeat along with wind and string instruments, and *ca tru*, which was sung by beautiful women to male nobles. A modern musical style called *nhac dan toc cai bien* combines traditional melodies with Western music.

After the Vietnam War, the Communist government tried to suppress popular rock music and romantic songs, which it condemned as too indulgent. But many Vietnamese people continued to listen to this music in private or at coffee shops and karaoke bars. The government has since loosened some restrictions on popular music. Vietnamese artists can now explore Western genres such as jazz, rock, and soul as well as combine them with Vietnamese lyrics and musical styles.

Vietnam's rich theatrical traditions still draw audiences today. Among the most popular theatrical experiences are *hat cheo* performances, which tell stories through folk songs, dancing, pantomime, acrobatics, and magic tricks. Originating in the court of the Ly and Tran dynasties, *hat tuong* performances incorporate many elements of classical Chinese opera. *Mua roi nuoc*, or water puppetry, is unique to Vietnam. Hidden puppeteers make stringed puppets dance along a stage of water, while singers provide the puppets' voices in a style associated with hat cheo.

Partly because of the lyrical sound of Vietnamese when spoken, poetry has always been important to the nation's literary traditions. Long ago, poems were passed down orally, but when Vietnam was ruled by China, poets began to write down their epic tales using Chinese characters. Among the greatest of these early writers was Nguyen Trai, who in the early 1400s

THE TALE OF KIEU

The Tale of Kieu is one of the greatest masterpieces of Vietnamese literature. This long narrative poem was written by Nguyen Du in the early 1800s. It tells of the challenges of a young woman as she tries to save the honor of her family. *The Tale of Kieu* remains so popular in Vietnam that many people have memorized the entire poem.

Vietnamese musicians playing traditional instruments may also wear traditional clothing during concerts.

wrote personal poems about everyday life. Another celebrated Vietnamese poet was Ho Xuan Huong, whose wit and wordplay were celebrated in the early 1800s and remain popular among contemporary readers.

By the 1930s, Vietnamese writers began to explore literary forms introduced by the French, such as the novel and the short story. While battling the French and Americans, tales of heroic revolutionaries were common. After reunification, the government endorsed a style known as socialist realism, which promoted the ideals of Communism.

MINI **BIO**

DUONG THU HUONG

Duong Thu Huong is among Vietnam's most famous and controversial writers. Born in North Vietnam in 1947, Huong volunteered to join the Communist Youth Brigade at age 20. She was sent to the front during the Vietnam War as part of a theater troupe that entertained injured soldiers.

After working in the film industry in Hanoi, Huong joined the Communist Party in 1985. The same year saw the publication of her first novel, *Beyond Illusions,* which became a bestseller in Vietnam. In 1987, she published her best-known book, *Paradise of the Blind,* to much success.

Huong later became disillusioned with the Communist regime and began speaking out against the corruption in its ranks. In 1989, she was expelled from the Communist Party, and in 1991, she was jailed for eight months without a trial. Since that time, her books have been banned in Vietnam, although translations of her works have earned a large readership abroad, especially in France and the United States. Her novels praised by foreign critics include *Novel Without a Name, No Man's Land,* and *The Zenith.* Vietnam's government has barred Huong from leaving the country.

Huong's book *Chon Vang*, which has the English title *No Man's Land*, sold more copies in France than J. K. Rowling's *Harry Potter and the Half-Blood Prince*.

By the late 1900s, the government decreased its restrictions on literature, allowing writers to explore a larger range of subjects. For instance, Nguyen Huy Thiep used his short stories to explore the tensions between rural and urban Vietnamese in the late 1900s. Most writers, however, still avoid the topic of politics out of fear of angering government officials.

CUISINE, HOLIDAYS, AND SPORTS

Like many aspects of Vietnamese culture, Vietnam's cuisine shows the influence of both Chinese and French traditions. Most dishes include either rice or noodles, and many feature fresh herbs and vegetables. Popular proteins include seafood, chicken, pork, duck, and tofu. Many dishes are seasoned with nuoc mam, a fish sauce also used for dipping. Food preferences vary slightly by region, with foods in the north tending to be salty and foods in the south more likely to incorporate spicy and sweet flavors. In central Vietnam, rice is less common and is often replaced by starches such as beans, corn, cassava, and sweet potatoes.

Throughout Vietnam, pho is a favorite food. This national dish is a soup of noodles and vegetables in chicken or beef broth, topped with meat or seafood. Other popular dishes include *cha gio*, deep-fried rice paper rolls filled with noodles, pork, crab, mushrooms, and onions; and *banh xeo*, a rice flour crepe filled with meat, shrimp, bean sprouts, and vegetables.

Banh chung, a rice cake filled with beans, pork, and peppers, is a treat Vietnamese people enjoy each year during Tet. Held during the full moon in late January or early February, this New Year celebration is the most important holiday in Vietnam. During its three days, people visit family

> **BANH MI**
>
> One of Vietnam's greatest contributions to world cuisine is the banh mi sandwich. The French introduced the Vietnamese to the baguette—a long, slim loaf of wheat bread that is crispy on the outside and soft in the middle. The French traditionally filled baguettes with a little butter and a layer of ham or pâté. But in the 1950s, a Vietnamese restaurant in what is now Ho Chi Minh City invented the banh mi by adding new ingredients. Today, banh mi sandwiches often include inventive and tasty combinations of pâté, pork or other proteins, herbs, pickled vegetables, chili peppers, and mayonnaise.

and friends and honor their ancestors by leaving food at their graves. Everyone wears new clothes, exchanges gifts, and gives thanks for the year ahead. Decorations made from red-and-gold paper, feasts of special foods, and firecrackers are all part of the festivities.

Many other national holidays mark historical events. The capture of Saigon, which later became Ho Chi Minh City, at the end of the Vietnam War is celebrated on April 30. The defeat of the French at Dien Bien Phu is commemorated on May 7. Vietnamese Independence Day is September 2, celebrating the day in 1945 that Ho Chi Minh announced the formation of the Democratic Republic of Vietnam. Both the birth and death of Ho are also important holidays observed on May 19 and September 3, respectively.

The Vietnamese enjoy watching and playing a variety of sports. The most popular sport is soccer, although the national team has found little success in international competitions. Young people play badminton, volleyball, and *sepak takraw*, a Southeast Asian sport that involves kicking a rattan ball over a net. Wrestling is a favorite spectator sport. The National Wrestling Championship holds matches across the country each spring. Other sports embraced by

Tran Hieu Ngan, *left*, competed in the women's 125-pound (57 kg) division of tae kwon do in the 2000 Olympics.

Vietnamese people include cycling, basketball, tennis, golf, and a variety of martial arts, including tae kwon do, judo, and karate.

Vietnam has sent athletes to the Summer Olympic Games since 1952. The country earned its first medal when tae kwon do fighter Tran Hieu Ngan took the silver in 2000. Vietnamese weightlifters won the silver medal in 2008 and the bronze in 2012. The nation's most successful Olympic athlete is marksman Hoang Xuan Vinh, who won gold and silver medals in shooting competitions at the 2016 Olympic games.

RELIGIOUS BELIEFS

As many as 86 percent of Vietnamese people say they practice no organized religion.[10] Although the constitution of Vietnam guarantees freedom of religion, the government heavily regulates and often harasses religious groups. While government suppression discourages religious practice, many Vietnamese remain strongly influenced by what are known as the three teachings: Buddhism, Taoism, and Confucianism. These three religions and philosophies were introduced to Vietnam by the Chinese many centuries ago, but they have since been reinterpreted in a way that makes them unique to Vietnam. These beliefs have also been intertwined with ancient local religions that involve worshipping spirits in the natural world.

Two religions practiced by a small minority had their origins in Vietnam in the early 1900s. Hoa Hao is a Buddhist sect that first developed in the Mekong River delta. Cao Dai, centered in Tay Ninh near Ho Chi Minh City, combines elements of Confucianism, Taoism, Buddhism, and

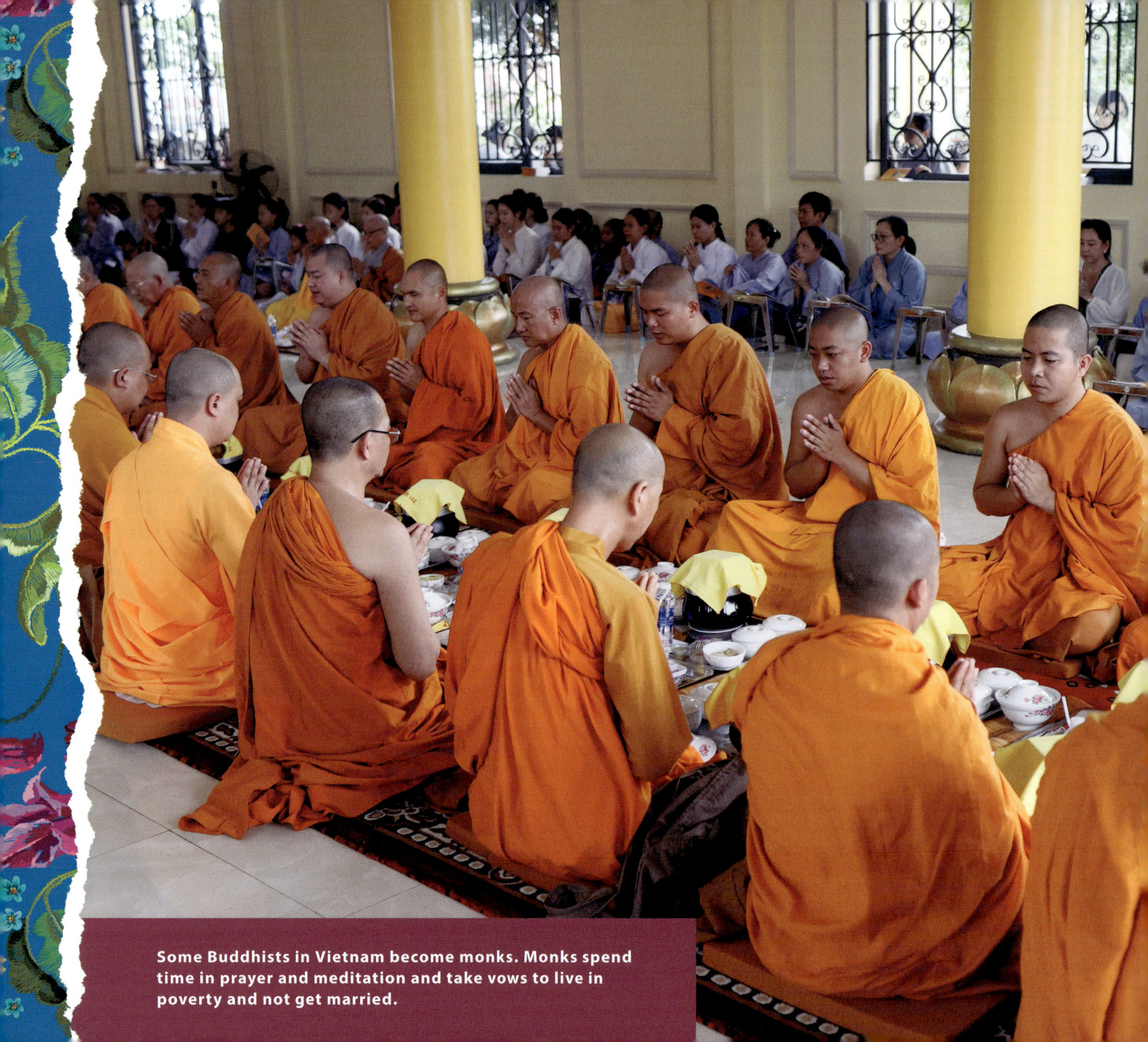

Some Buddhists in Vietnam become monks. Monks spend time in prayer and meditation and take vows to live in poverty and not get married.

Roman Catholicism. Its followers believe they commune with the spirits of religious leaders, such as Jesus and the Buddha, as well as historical figures, such as French national heroine Joan of Arc and film comedian Charlie Chaplin. Both Hoa Hao and Cao Dai are growing in popularity.

Most Christians in Vietnam are Roman Catholics. Many Catholics left the country as refugees following the Vietnam War. Those who remain are largely clustered in cities in the south. Other Christian religions observed include the Churches of Christ, the Evangelical Church of Vietnam—South, and the Church of Jesus Christ of Latter-Day Saints. Very small populations within Vietnam practice Islam, Hinduism, Brahmanism, Baha'i, and Judaism.

CHAPTER **SIX**

POLITICS

Ever since Vietnam was reunified in 1975, it has been a Communist nation. Communism is a political ideology first supported by the German philosopher Karl Marx in the 1800s. It holds that property should not be owned privately. Instead, all citizens of a nation should communally control the industries and natural resources. The government determines prices and wages. Most Communist countries have only one political party, which does not allow citizens to criticize the government.

Today, Vietnam is one of only a handful of Communist countries. In the 1900s, many Communist regimes collapsed because their policies could not produce a functional economy. Communism in Vietnam survived because it abandoned some Communist economic theories, which allowed its economy to grow.

Busts of Ho Chi Minh stand in government buildings in Vietnam.

The Communist Party of Vietnam (CPV), however, has retained near-complete control over the political and social arenas.

THE FOUR PILLARS

The fourth article of Vietnam's constitution holds that "the Communist Party of Vietnam . . . is the leading force of the State and society."[1] Almost all leaders in the Vietnamese government are required to be members of the CPV. Every five years the party holds a convention, during which elected delegates select 200 members for the Central Committee. The Central Committee then elects the 18-person Politburo, the top decision-making body of the party. Another important part of the CPV is the Fatherland Front, a group of political associations that promote the party's policies, train potential leaders, and form lists of candidates for the National Assembly, Vietnam's lawmaking body.

The most powerful position in the government's executive branch is the party's head, known as the general secretary. Unlike in most Communist governments, the party leader is not a dictator who rules alone. Instead, Vietnam's central leadership is shared by four officials known as the

THE FLAG OF VIETNAM

Vietnam's bold flag features a large five-pointed yellow star in the center of a bright red field. It was adopted on September 29, 1945, after the Democratic Republic of Vietnam in the northern region declared its independence. The red field stands for the blood shed by citizens to free themselves from foreign domination. The five points of the star symbolize five groups within their population: peasants, workers, intellectuals, traders, and soldiers.

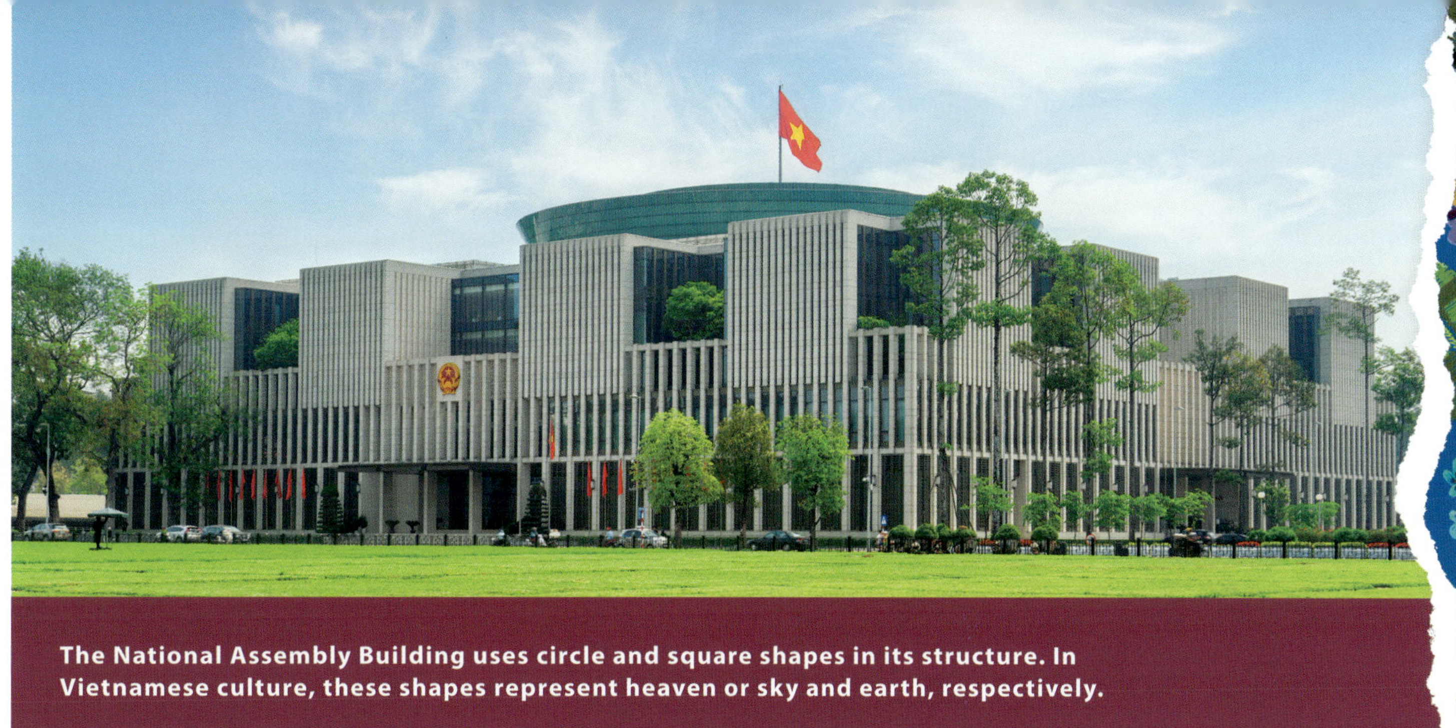

The National Assembly Building uses circle and square shapes in its structure. In Vietnamese culture, these shapes represent heaven or sky and earth, respectively.

four pillars. In addition to the general secretary, they include the president, the prime minister, and the chairperson of the National Assembly.

As head of state, the president's position is largely ceremonial, although the president commands the armed forces and chairs the National Defense and Security Council. The president is elected to a five-year term by the National Assembly. However, as with the appointment of all members of the four pillars, the Politburo has great influence over the selection process. The president makes recommendations for the vice president, prime minister, and chief justice of the Supreme People's Court, which the National Assembly then votes to confirm.

The prime minister is the head of government, taking charge of its day-to-day operations. This official is assisted by deputy prime ministers and cabinet ministers, whom the prime minister

Issues the National Assembly votes on include approving the construction of high-speed railways.

nominates and the National Assembly approves. Each minister is responsible for overseeing an aspect of the government, such as foreign affairs, finance, health, justice, public security, transport, and industry and trade.

THE NATIONAL ASSEMBLY

The National Assembly is Vietnam's single-chamber legislative body. Its 500 members meet twice a year to pass laws, which are initiated by officials in the executive branch. Historically, the assembly members merely approved legislation promoted by the leadership of the CPV. In recent years, however, they have sometimes pushed back against the party's policies and tried to exert more influence over national lawmaking.

The Vietnamese government reported that 99 percent of its 67.5 million registered voters voted in the 2016 national election.[7]

Elections for National Assembly members are held every five years following the CPV convention. Many candidates are members of the Politburo and Central Committee selected during the convention. All citizens who are 18 or older are eligible to vote. The CPV controls all aspects of elections and says that almost every eligible voter casts a ballot. A US State Department report from 2022 said that Vietnam's national election in 2021 was "neither free nor fair," because of the control exerted by the CPV and the country's refusal to allow outside voting rights groups to monitor the voting.[2]

Since 1992, people who are not members of the Communist Party have been permitted to run for the National Assembly. All independent candidates, however, must be approved by the Fatherland Front to appear on the ballot. In 2021, there were 74 independent candidates out of a field of 868.[3] They included activists, journalists, legal reformers, and human rights workers. The election also featured the first openly gay candidate, although he lost his bid. Only 14 assembly seats were won by independents.[4]

In 2021, female candidates won 151 seats to make up 30 percent of the National Assembly.[5] By law, the party sets a target for women to make up 35 percent of assembly candidates.[6] As a result, Vietnam's legislature has one of the highest proportions of female legislators of any Asian country.

LOCAL GOVERNMENTS

Vietnam is divided into 64 provinces, five of which are municipalities. The municipalities are Can Tho, Da Nang, Haiphong, Hanoi, and Ho Chi Minh City. Each province and municipality is governed by an elected People's Council. Select members of each council form the People's Committee, which runs the day-to-day operations of the provincial and municipal governments.

Below provinces, Vietnam has two more tiers of local government. The second is the district level, which includes several dozen urban districts and hundreds of rural districts. The third is the commune level, which includes about 10,000 communities.[8] Both districts and communes have People's Councils and People's Committees. At all levels, local governments are under the strict control of the national government. Candidates for local councils are screened by the CPV to ensure their party loyalty.

"THE SONG OF THE MARCHING TROOPS"

During the August Revolution of 1945, many participants sang the rousing song "Tien Quan Ca," or "The Song of the Marching Troops," which is now Vietnam's national anthem. Its lyrics celebrate Vietnamese soldiers' victories on the battlefield against their foes. Van Cao, a composer, poet, and painter, wrote the music and lyrics. The year after his death in 1995, he was awarded the Ho Chi Minh Prize by the government for his contributions to Vietnamese culture.

THE JUDICIARY AND THE MILITARY

Vietnam's judicial system has courts at most levels of government. The highest court is the Supreme People's Court, which is composed of a chief justice and 13 other judges. They are recommended to the court by the president and elected to five-year terms by the National Assembly. In addition to hearing cases, the Supreme Court supervises local People's Courts at the provincial and district levels. The chief justice can also request that the National Assembly establish special tribunals for cases dealing with important national issues, such as treason.

Vietnam's constitution maintains that judges operate independently. But in practice, they are under the tight control of party leaders. Judges must prove their loyalty to the CPV to obtain and keep their positions.

The People's Army of Vietnam, one of the largest and most powerful militaries in Southeast Asia, is also deeply intertwined in Communist Party politics. It is overseen by the Central Military Commission, which is led by the party's general secretary. Serving in the military as a senior officer is often a path to membership in the Central Committee and the Politburo.

Vietnam's armed forces include an army, navy, air force, border defense force, and coast guard. Young men between the ages of 18 and 27 are drafted to serve two or three years. Military service for women is voluntary.

FIGHTING CORRUPTION

In all areas of the Vietnamese government, corruption has long been rampant. Salaries for government workers are often so low that workers resort to taking bribes to survive. Fearing that widespread corruption was damaging the Communist Party, general secretary Nguyen Phu Trong began an anti-corruption campaign called Blazing Furnaces in 2016.

To Lam was sworn in as president on May 22, 2024.

The scope of the campaign grew considerably in the 2020s as it was implemented by Minister of Public Security To Lam. He oversaw thousands of arrests, firings, and resignations of government officials, including many at the highest levels of power. By 2024, nearly half of the members of the Politburo elected in 2021 had lost their positions.[9]

The Blazing Furnaces campaign even led to the resignations of two presidents—Nguyen Xuan Phuc in January 2023 and Vo Van Thuong in 2024. Both were accused of violating Communist rule, another name for corruption. Their resignations marked the first time members of the four pillars had stepped down since Vietnam's reunification in 1975.

After President Thuong's resignation, Lam became the new president. This led some to conclude that, as the head of public security, he had been motivated less by eliminating corruption and more by a desire to eliminate political rivals. Lam became even more powerful when he was named general secretary of the Communist Party following Trong's death in 2024.

POLITICAL REPRESSION

Another political issue that has long plagued Vietnam is the Communist Party's response to criticism, which has made Vietnam one of the more repressive countries in the world. Critics of the party and the government are subject to detention without trial. Political prisoners are often beaten by the police during interrogation. Some have died in custody.

To appease foreign trading partners concerned about Vietnam's poor human rights record, the government grew somewhat more tolerant of free speech for a time. But the 2020s saw a crackdown on citizens' rights and freedoms as Lam's allies came to dominate the Politburo. Starting in late 2023, dozens of journalists, environmentalists, and labor rights advocates were arrested, and many organizations seeking to hold the government accountable were shut down or outlawed.

A SCANDALOUS STEAK

In late 2021, a video was widely shared by Vietnamese internet users. It showed To Lam—then the minister of public security—in an upscale London restaurant being hand-fed steak covered in gold specks by a celebrity chef. The Vietnamese public was outraged that a leader of the Communist Party was enjoying luxuries unavailable to the vast majority of Vietnamese citizens, especially after COVID-19 hurt the nation's economy. Authorities responded to the scandal by sentencing an activist who posted a parody video to more than five years in prison.

CHAPTER **SEVEN**

ECONOMICS

When Vietnam was reunified in 1975, the nation was suffering from the devastation of the Vietnam War. Most of its people were living in poverty. Since then, the country has seen a reversal of fortune. In 2023, Vietnam's gross domestic product (GDP)—the value of goods and services produced by the country during one year—totaled more than $1.3 trillion.[1]

Less than 5 percent of Vietnamese people now live below the poverty line, with the poor largely concentrated in remote rural areas.[2] Most citizens are moderately prosperous, with good financial prospects for the future. With one of the fastest-growing economies in Asia, the Vietnamese government aims to join the ranks of the world's wealthiest nations in just a few decades.

Vietnam's forests can be harvested for resources, but they also support the tourism industry. People can stroll along the Golden Bridge in Da Nang to get stunning views of mountainous forests.

THE RISE OF INDUSTRY

Much of Vietnam's prosperity is the product of the government's concentration on growing its industrial sector. Since the mid-1980s, it has largely abandoned the Communist ideal of businesses owned and operated by the state. Instead, it attracts international corporations and foreign investment. In recent years, it has also benefited from tensions between the United States and China.

US companies have long manufactured in China to cut costs. But the companies are increasingly concerned about Chinese government policies affecting their operations, especially after China imposed severe lockdowns in 2020 during the early COVID-19 pandemic. Vietnam presents a welcome alternative for manufacturing. Apple and Nike are two large US corporations that manufacture goods in Vietnam.

Many foreign companies also operate in Vietnam because of the available workforce. With a reputation for being hardworking, diligent, and well-educated, Vietnam's laborers are an attractive economic asset. And because of the low cost of

THE VIETNAMESE DONG

The State Bank of Vietnam issues the nation's currency, the dong. Banknotes of various amounts are different colors, but all show a portrait of Ho Chi Minh on the front side. On the back are pictures of famous landmarks such as the Temple of Literature and Hoi An pagoda bridge, or notable locations such as Ha Long Bay and the Nha Rong Port. The highest denomination is 500,000 dongs.[3] This note was worth about $20 in 2024.[4]

living in Vietnam, employing a Vietnamese worker is often half the cost of employing a Chinese laborer from China's coastal region.

Most Vietnamese factories are located in Hanoi and Ho Chi Minh City. Goods manufactured there include processed foods, beverages, clothing, shoes, machinery, glass, tires, and paper products. Because of its limestone resources, Vietnam is a leading producer of cement. Steel and chemical fertilizer manufacturing is a growing part of its economy. Other newly important industrial products include electronic equipment, automobiles, and motorcycles. Increasingly, Ho Chi Minh City is becoming a technology center as foreign investment builds up Vietnam's semiconductor industry.

AGRICULTURE

Traditionally, most Vietnamese people made their living by working small farms. In the early 2000s, industry replaced agriculture as Vietnam's main source of economic wealth, but farming is still important. Agriculture employs about half of Vietnam's workers and accounts for many of its most profitable exports.[5]

Rice is Vietnam's most important crop. It is cultivated in irrigated paddies in the Red and Mekong River deltas. Vietnam is the third-largest rice exporter in the world, bested only by India and Thailand.[6]

Other important food crops grown in Vietnam include corn, cassava, cashews, peanuts, and sweet potatoes. Fruit trees produce bananas, coconuts, oranges, mangoes, and jackfruits. In the central highlands, coffee, tea, sugarcane, and tobacco are grown on large plantations. Rubber tree plantations, originally established by the French, have made Vietnam one of the leading suppliers of rubber.

Small farms often raise livestock, such as cattle, hogs, chicken, and ducks. These farms produce a variety of animal products, including pork, beef, poultry, buffalo meat, eggs, milk, and cattle hides. Draft animals, especially water buffalo, play an important role in rice farming.

FISHING, FORESTRY, AND MINING

With its long coastline and many interior lakes and rivers, Vietnam has a vibrant fishing industry. Along the shore, fishers catch shrimp, squid, crabs, and lobsters. The Mekong River delta holds freshwater fish, while fish farms yield carp, tilapia, and prawns.

Despite deforestation due to pesticides and the conversion of forests into farmland, forestry remains a significant part of Vietnam's economy. Factories transform the nation's forests into paper, pulp, plywood, and lumber. Wooden furniture is also an important export product.

FLOATING MARKETS OF THE MEKONG

Before modern roads and bridges, it was difficult to travel through the Mekong River delta during flood season. For daily shopping, people boarded boats and visited a floating market. Vendors in boats line waterways to sell fresh fruits and vegetables, handicrafts, and household goods. They often hoist an example of their wares on tall poles so buyers can see what they are selling from a distance. Although people in the delta now have more buying options, the floating markets remain popular both with locals and tourists.

Although Vietnam is rich in mineral resources, its mining industry is underdeveloped. In the north are large deposits of lime, phosphates, tin, zinc, lead, gold, and gemstones. Northern reserves of coal provide a common energy source. Offshore oil deposits lie in the South China Sea, but territorial disputes with China have prevented Vietnam from fully developing them.

EXPORTS, IMPORTS, AND THE SERVICE SECTOR

In the early 2000s, the Vietnamese government developed industries that produce goods for export. Exported goods include petroleum, rice, clothing, shoes, textiles, coffee, rubber, fish, and shellfish. The United States is the biggest market for Vietnamese exports. China, South Korea, Japan, and Hong Kong are also important export partners.

Vietnam had about 27,490 square miles (71,200 sq km) of planted rice paddies in 2023. Agriculture as a whole accounts for 12 percent of Vietnam's GDP.

Basket boat tours are popular in the coconut forest at Hoi An.

Even as many Vietnamese industries are growing, the country must still import some products to meet consumer demand. Imported goods include cotton, electronics, machinery, steel products, and vehicles. Most imports come from China, South Korea, Japan, Taiwan, and Thailand.

The total goods exported by Vietnam in 2023 were worth $374 billion.[8]

With increased urbanization, providing services has become an important part of the economy. Service industries include government, education, banking, retail sales, communications, consumer services, and insurance. Tourism is one growing service industry. In addition to hotel workers, restaurant staff, and tour guides, the tourism industry employs street vendors who sell food, electronics, jewelry, and other goods to mainly foreign travelers visiting Vietnam's cities. Most tourists are from China, South Korea, and the United States.

GETTING AROUND

Vietnam's geography makes land travel between the north and south challenging. The country is narrow at its center. In this central region, mountains to the west force most roads and railways to crowd along a narrow coastal corridor. Most traffic must travel through this narrow area. The country continues to expand its roads and railways.

Although car ownership is on the rise, many households do not have one. Most people instead use motorbikes to travel throughout the country or within cities. In Ho Chi Minh City alone, some seven million motorbikes clog the streets and fill the air with exhaust.[7] Hanoi has voted to ban motorbikes by 2030, but without adequate public transportation, the public remains devoted to these vehicles as their favored mode of transportation.

In the Red and Mekong River deltas, locals often travel by boat on rivers and canals. Goods are also transported on small barges along these waterways. Larger ships are found at major ports, such as Haiphong, Da Nang, and Ho Chi Minh City.

Vietnam has 42 airports, including international airports at Hanoi, Ho Chi Minh City, and Da Nang.[9] Several airlines operate in the country, including the state-owned Vietnam Airlines. To aid tourism, the airline offers international as well as domestic flights, with an increasing number of direct flights to and from Europe and North America.

ECONOMIC CHALLENGES

Despite Vietnam's thriving economy, the country faces several problems that threaten its prosperity. Its aging infrastructure limits the productivity of its industrial sector. The country's ports and airports need upgrading, and many of its roads are in disrepair. Roads in rural areas are often unpaved and subject to blockage by landslides. These challenges slow traffic.

A CORRUPT TYCOON

One of the most brazen criminals snared by the Vietnamese government's recent anti-corruption campaign was real estate tycoon Truong My Lan. She was charged with stealing from the Saigon Commercial Bank and bribing officials to help cover up the theft. Found guilty of causing financial damages totaling $20 billion, she was sentenced to death by a panel of judges in 2024.[10] Before the banking scandal broke, Truong My Lan had been one of the wealthiest women in Vietnam.

In 2024, there were more than 77 million registered motorbikes in Vietnam.

Vietnam has made great strides in electrifying remote areas. Nearly all rural homes now have electricity, while in 1993 only 14 percent did.[11] However, the demand for electrical power for industrial facilities has far outpaced the available supply. Although the country has been constructing new hydroelectric plants, electrical power often goes out unexpectedly.

Widespread corruption has long added to the cost of doing business in Vietnam. The government's recent anti-corruption campaign has curbed the routine bribery of officials. But it has also created roadblocks for new industrial and infrastructure projects. Such projects often need the approval of officials in as many as a dozen ministries. Many officials now refuse to grant these approvals for fear of getting caught up in an anti-corruption investigation and losing their positions. Instead, they prefer to approve nothing, making it more difficult for Vietnam to achieve the upgrades its economy needs.

CHAPTER **EIGHT**

VIETNAM TODAY

Vietnam's cities are full of high skyscrapers, streets are jammed with traffic, and sidewalks are full of hurrying pedestrians. But for most Vietnamese people, the pace of life is much less hectic. Although modern devices such as televisions and smartphones are common, in many ways daily life for the majority of the population, which lives in rural areas, is not so different from that of their ancestors.

The lives of many rural Vietnamese revolve around the growing of crops, especially rice. Their social contacts are largely restricted to their family and others who live in their small villages. Housing in villages varies, but most homes are built with materials easily gathered from the surroundings. In the chilly north,

In addition to protection from flooding and predators, stilt houses offer more airflow because of their height, helping to keep the house cool.

Ao dai is the national dress of Vietnam. There are many modern takes on this traditional dress, which can be worn by women and men and is distinguished by its front and back flaps.

people live in houses made of wood or bamboo with tiled roofs. In the hot south, homes are built from straw, thatch, or palm leaves. The foundations of houses along rivers or in the highlands are often built on stilts to protect residents from floodwaters and wild animals. As the incomes of rural families rise, some replace traditional houses with ones made of stone, brick, and concrete.

Rural homes are small, usually having only one or two rooms. The furnishings include beds made from wood or bamboo covered with a reed mat. At a low table, families share meals while seated on the floor.

Often, the family home includes an altar, where members can worship their ancestors. Many homes have no running water. But nearly all have electricity thanks to an aggressive electrification program launched by the government in the late 1990s.

AO DAI

Featuring a long, slit tunic worn over loose-fitting trousers, the ao dai is the traditional national outfit of Vietnam. It is derived from a style of dress involving five garments from Vietnam's royal court of the 1700s. The ao dai took its present two-garment form in the 1930s, when artist Lemur Nguyen Cat Tuong designed an ao dai collection for the wife of Vietnam's last emperor. The ao dai is now usually reserved for weddings and other special occasions, although female high school students must wear it at least one day a week.

For both men and women in the countryside, the standard clothing is baggy pants with loose-fitting shirts or blouses. Women's clothing is often adorned with colorful embroidery. People usually wear sandals and large conical straw hats that protect them from the sun.

LIVING IN CITIES

In recent decades, many Vietnamese have moved from the countryside to cities in search of better jobs and higher pay. This influx has caused an urban housing crisis because the amount of available housing has not kept up with the demand. Families often have no choice but to crowd into small apartments. Sometimes family members of two or three generations must share a single room. Most of the urban housing available is apartments in multistory buildings made from brick or concrete.

City dwellers, however, do have access to bustling commercial neighborhoods. While villagers generally buy food and other goods at small family-owned stalls, people in cities can shop at malls, department stores, and supermarkets. Urban streets are also full of casual food stalls, cafés, and entertainment venues.

In cities, people usually wear clothing similar to that of North Americans and Europeans. Men wear light-colored shirts with dark trousers, while most women dress in blouses and skirts. Clothing is made of lightweight materials to help people withstand the heat and humidity.

IN THE FAMILY

Both in cities and in the countryside, family is very important to most Vietnamese people. Family ties tend to be close, and extended families often live and work together. Extended families can include grandparents, aunts, uncles, and first and second cousins.

Family members have a sense of obligation to one another, and they generally value what is good for the family more than their own personal preferences. The father is considered the head of the family. If he is away, the eldest male child takes over that role. Wives are usually expected to submit to their husbands, but they are often in charge of decisions about child-rearing and household finances. In addition to their domestic responsibilities, more than half of women work outside the home.[1]

THE NAME NGUYEN

About 40 percent of Vietnamese people have the surname Nguyen, which, according to the country's naming system, appears before one's personal name. Its popularity is probably due to Nguyen being the name of Vietnam's last dynasty, which ruled from 1802 to 1945. Taking the name was likely a way for Vietnamese subjects to show their loyalty to the ruling family. Today, Nguyen is common not only in Vietnam but also in several other countries where Vietnamese immigrants live. It is the thirteenth-most-common surname in Australia and among the 100 most common in the United States, France, and Canada.[2]

Children are highly valued, but they are expected to contribute to the family. In rural areas, boys and girls help with farmwork, gardening, and caring for livestock. In cities, they assist their mothers with chores, care for younger siblings, run errands, or hold part-time jobs to boost the family income.

Family elders are respected for their wisdom. Traditionally, their long life was celebrated at a party held for their fortieth birthday, but as life expectancy has risen, this event is more likely to be held when they turn 70, 80, or 90. After elders die, the families hold ceremonies on certain anniversaries of their deaths as part of a practice known as ancestor worship.

Vietnamese people usually eat three meals a day, with dinner being the main meal. Many people grab daytime meals and snacks at food stalls, but the evening meal is generally eaten at home with family. Diners sit on mats on the floor

Children may begin helping their parents with farmwork from a young age.

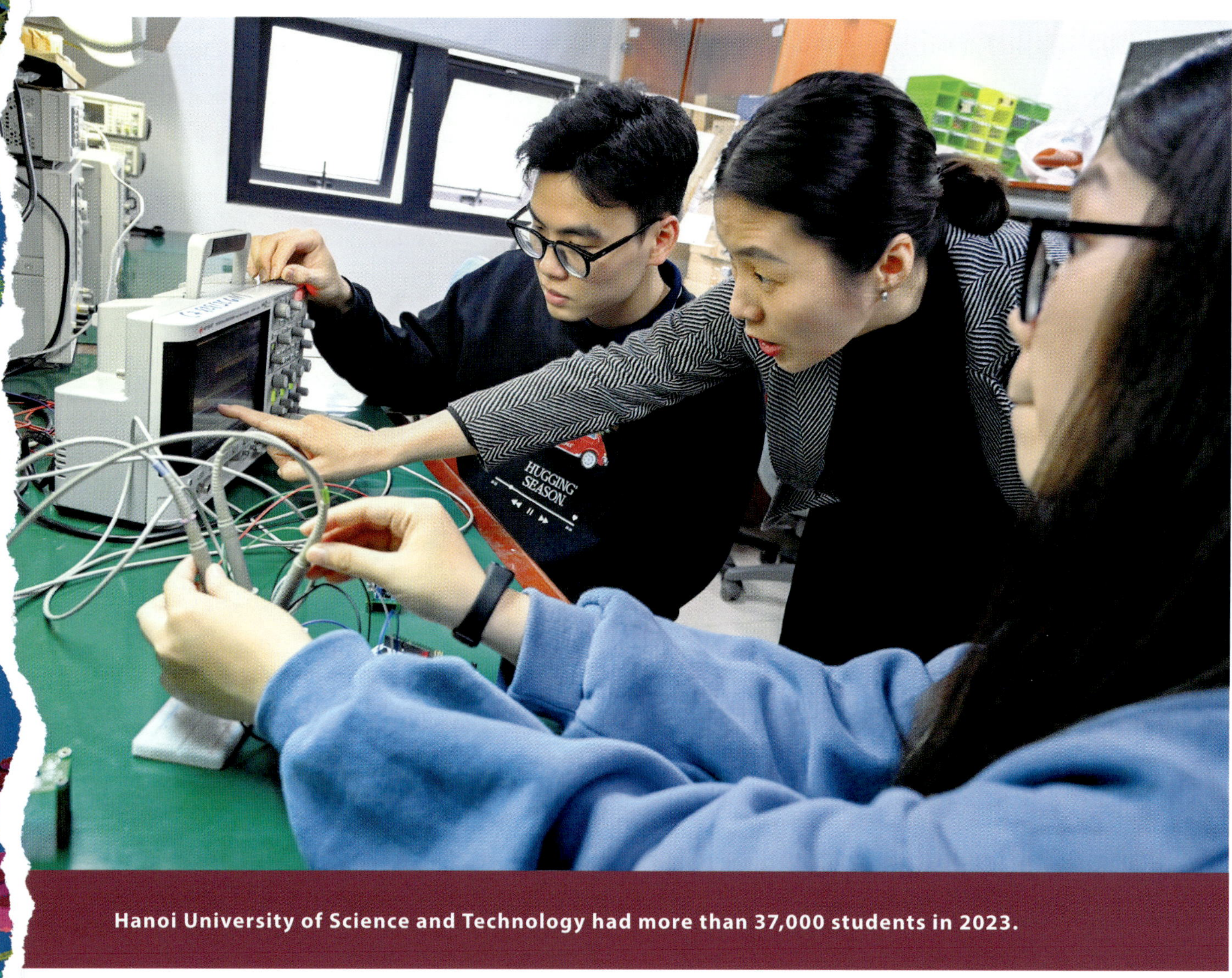

Hanoi University of Science and Technology had more than 37,000 students in 2023.

by the dinner table, each holding a bowl of rice and a pair of chopsticks. They alternate between taking a bite of rice with a bite from communal bowls of other foods on the table. A typical meal might include vegetables cooked in fermented sauce with small portions of meat or seafood.

EDUCATION AND HEALTH

Between the ages of six and ten, Vietnamese children are required to attend primary school, which is financed by the government. Seven additional years of secondary education are also free, but many students drop out after primary school. Some cannot afford the books they need to continue their education. In rural areas, children are often forced to leave school because their help is needed on their family's farm.

Vietnam's system of higher education includes universities, technical institutes, business academies, and agricultural colleges. Among the largest are Hanoi University of Science and Technology, Vietnam National University, and Can Tho University. Despite increased government spending on education in the early 2000s, these schools do not have enough openings to meet the demand for higher education. Each year thousands of university students travel abroad, mostly to the United States and Japan, to attend school.

Ninety-six percent of all Vietnamese people age 15 or older can read and write in at least one language.[3]

The government of Vietnam provides free health care to its citizens. The health-care system has helped increase life expectancy, reduce infant mortality, and manage the COVID-19 pandemic through widespread vaccination. But the country continues to experience health-care challenges, including malnutrition in rural regions and a high risk of serious diseases, such as dengue fever, malaria, and typhoid fever. Government health-care funding has not kept up with population growth, meaning it cannot cover the medical care for all citizens, leaving many people to resort to traditional folk remedies because they cannot afford modern medicine.

RECREATION AND MEDIA

During their leisure time, Vietnamese people enjoy a wide range of sports and games. Soccer, volleyball, badminton, tennis, and cycling are popular, especially among young people. Many people practice tai chi, a Chinese martial art, to stay fit. Favorite games include billiards, chess, and mah-jongg. Outdoor activities include taking evening walks through urban parks and swimming in lakes, rivers, and the ocean.

At home, people often relax by watching television and listening to the radio. They also read a variety of newspapers, most of which are in Vietnamese, although a few are published in English, Chinese, or French. Recently, the internet has become a popular source of entertainment and information.

All media in Vietnam, however, is subject to government censorship. Radio and television stations are owned by the government and managed by the Ministry of Culture Information, ensuring that broadcasts show support for the Communist regime. Print media is also highly regulated, and any journalist who criticizes the government faces harassment, fines, or prison time. The internet is not as tightly monitored, although many websites are blocked. Internet users are often arrested for voicing anti-government sentiments.

SUOI TIEN THEME PARK

Just south of Ho Chi Minh City is the Suoi Tien Theme Park, a vast amusement park with Vietnamese history, folklore, and Buddhist beliefs as its theme. The attraction has employees dressed as golden monkeys and is filled with sculptures of tortoises, phoenixes, and dragons. One giant dragon holds a shrine to the Buddha in its mouth. Visitors can paddle through a lake in dog-shaped boats and feed live crocodiles raw meat from a fishing rod. They can also slip down waterslides emerging from the sculpted heads of 12-story-high Buddhist sages.[4]

GOING FORWARD

Dealing with government censors is just one of many challenges the citizens of Vietnam face. The country needs solutions to an array of problems, including human rights abuses, government corruption, inadequate infrastructure, endangered wildlife, climate change, pollution, and income inequity. But when activists speak up about these threats, the government tends to silence rather than listen.

In recent decades, however, the government has made some decisions that have improved the lives of many of its people. Leaders have restored relations with many foreign countries. This has brought lucrative trade partnerships and helped

In Vietnamese cities, people have access to many restaurants to meet friends and enjoy a meal.

the country remain in the good graces of both the United States and China, even as tensions rise between these powers. Additionally, the government's economic reforms have turned Vietnam into one of the most dynamic economies in the world. Once mired in poverty, the average Vietnamese citizen now enjoys a better living standard than ever before.

One quality of the Vietnamese character likely to have a great impact on the nation's future is resilience. A relentlessly forward-looking people, the Vietnamese have faced many serious difficulties posed by foreign enemies and internal disputes throughout their history. But they have always been able to find new ways to survive and ultimately thrive in changing and challenging times, all the while remaining true to themselves and their country.

ESSENTIAL **FACTS**

OFFICIAL NAME: SOCIALIST REPUBLIC OF VIETNAM

GEOGRAPHY

Area: 127,881 square miles (331,210 sq km)

Highest Elevation: Fan Si Peak at 10,315 feet (3,144 m)

Lowest Elevation: South China Sea at 0 feet (0 m)

PEOPLE

Population: 105.8 million (2024 est.)

Most Populous City: Ho Chi Minh City (9.3 million)

Ethnic Groups: Mostly Kinh (ethnic Vietnamese); also Tay, Tai, Muong, Khmer, Hmong, and Nung

Religions: Mostly unaffiliated; some Roman Catholicism, Buddhism, and Protestantism

GOVERNMENT

Type of Government: Communist party–led state

Capital: Hanoi

Head of State: President

Head of Government: Prime minister

Legislature: Unicameral with a National Assembly

ECONOMY

Currency: Dong

Major Industries: Food processing, mining, garments, shoes, machinery, steel, cement, chemical fertilizer, glass, tires, oil, and mobile phones

Natural Resources: Antimony, phosphates, coal, manganese, rare earth elements, bauxite, chromate, timber, hydropower, arable land, and offshore oil and gas deposits

NATIONAL SYMBOLS

National Anthem: “Tien Quan Ca” (“The Song of the Marching Troops”)

National Motto: Independence, Freedom, and Happiness

National Flower: Lotus blossom

GLOSSARY

black market
The illegal trade of goods that are banned or scarce.

colony
A country or region controlled by the leaders of another country.

Communism
A political system in which the government controls the economy and owns all property.

deciduous
Shedding leaves yearly.

delegate
A person selected to represent a group of people.

dredge
To dig or deepen a waterway by removing earth from the bottom of that body of water.

dynasty
A succession of rulers from the same family.

guerrilla
An independent fighter in a war who is not part of a regular army.

industrialization
Wide-scale development of manufacturing and other industries.

infrastructure
The physical structures, such as roads, railways, and power plants, that make it possible for a city or nation to function.

missionary
A person sent to promote a religion, often Christianity, or to operate a service such as a school or hospital under that religion, usually where that religion is not widely practiced.

pagoda
A tower with many stories, each with its own roof, often built as part of a Buddhist temple.

pâté
A paste or finely chopped mixture of meat.

plantation
A large farm worked by laborers who live on the grounds.

plateau
An area of level ground that is higher than the surrounding area.

ADDITIONAL **RESOURCES**

SELECTED BIBLIOGRAPHY

Jamieson, Neil L., et al. "Vietnam." *Britannica*, 27 Nov. 2024, britannica.com. Accessed 27 Nov. 2024.

Scott, Patrick. "36 Hours: Ho Chi Minh City, Vietnam." *New York Times*, 3 Aug. 2023, nytimes.com. Accessed 27 Nov. 2024.

Stewart, Iain, et al. *Vietnam*. Lonely Planet, 2023.

Vietnam & Angkor Wat. Rev. ed., DK Eyewitness Travel, 2014.

FURTHER READINGS

Farrell, Mary Cronk. *Close-Up on War: The Story of Pioneering Photojournalist Catherine Leroy in Vietnam*. Amulet, 2022.

Pham, Thien. *Family Style: Memories of an American from Vietnam*. First Second, 2023.

Seah, Audrey, et al. *Vietnam*. 4th ed., Cavendish Square, 2024.

ONLINE RESOURCES

To learn more about Vietnam, please visit **abdobooklinks.com** or scan this QR code. These links are routinely monitored and updated to provide the most current information available.

MORE INFORMATION

For more information on this subject, contact or visit the following organizations:

Embassy of the Socialist Republic of Vietnam

1233 20th St. NW, Ste. 400
Washington, DC 20036
vietnamembassy-usa.org

Vietnam's US embassy represents Vietnam's interests in the United States. Its website has information about the nation.

Vietnam National Museum of History

No. 1 Trang Tien
No. 216 Tran Quang Khai
Hoan Kiem, Hanoi
Vietnam
baotanglichsu.vn/vi

With more than 200,000 documents and artifacts, the Vietnam National Museum of History highlights the country's history from the prehistoric era to the present day.

Vietnamese Heritage Museum

13962 Seaboard Cir.
Garden Grove, CA 92843
vietnamesemuseum.org

The Vietnamese Heritage Museum seeks to preserve the history of Vietnamese refugees in the United States by collecting oral testimonies and artifacts.

SOURCE **NOTES**

CHAPTER 1. A TOUR OF VIETNAM

1. "San Francisco to Hanoi." *United Airlines*, n.d., united.com. Accessed 7 Feb. 2025.
2. "Flight Time from Hanoi to Hue." *Trip.com*, n.d., trip.com. Accessed 7 Feb. 2025.
3. "Explore Hue Imperial Cuisine (Ẩm thực cung đình Huế)." *Vietnamese Language Studies*, 22 Jan. 2024, vlstudies.com. Accessed 7 Feb. 2025.
4. "Vietnam." *CIA World Factbook*, 5 Feb. 2025, cia.gov. Accessed 7 Feb. 2025.
5. Patrick Scott. "36 Hours: Ho Chi Minh City, Vietnam." *New York Times*, 3 Aug. 2023, nytimes.com. Accessed 7 Feb. 2025.

CHAPTER 2. GEOGRAPHY

1. "Vietnam." *CIA World Factbook*, 5 Feb. 2025, cia.gov. Accessed 7 Feb. 2025.
2. "Vietnam."
3. "Geography." *Embassy of the Socialist Republic of Vietnam*, n.d., vietnamembassy-usa.org. Accessed 7 Feb. 2025.
4. Benjamin Elisha Sawe. "Longest Rivers in Vietnam." *WorldAtlas*, 25 Apr. 2017, worldatlas.com. Accessed 7 Feb. 2025.
5. "The Emerald Isles of Ha Long Bay." *NASA Earth Observatory*, 7 May 2022, earthobservatory.nasa.gov. Accessed 7 Feb. 2025.
6. Ronald J. Cima, editor. *Vietnam: A Country Study*. Library of Congress, 1989. 86.
7. Cima, *Vietnam*, 89.
8. "Vietnam."
9. Cima, *Vietnam*, 89.
10. *Worldmark Encyclopedia of Cultures and Daily Life: Asia & Oceania*. 3rd ed., Gale, 2017. 1303.
11. Damien Cave. "Hanoi Floods as Landslides and Rising Rivers Push Typhoon Death Toll to 143." *New York Times*, 11 Sept. 2024, nytimes.com. Accessed 7 Feb. 2025.
12. "Vietnam."
13. "Planning a Trip to Vietnam." *Frommer's*, n.d., frommers.com. Accessed 7 Feb. 2025.
14. "Vietnam's Central Highlands Travel Guide." *Frommer's*, n.d., frommers.com. Accessed 7 Feb. 2025.
15. "Planning a Trip to Vietnam."

CHAPTER 3. PLANTS AND ANIMALS

1. "Saola." *Animalia*, n.d., animalia.bio. Accessed 7 Feb. 2025.
2. "Vietnam." *CIA World Factbook*, 5 Feb. 2025, cia.gov. Accessed 7 Feb. 2025.
3. Stephen Nash. "Vietnam's Empty Forests." *New York Times*, 1 Apr. 2019, nytimes.com. Accessed 7 Feb. 2025.
4. "Vietnam."
5. "US, Vietnamese Science Agencies Partner to Protect Biodiversity in Vietnam." *US Geological Survey*, 3 Sept. 2016, usgs.gov. Accessed 7 Feb. 2025.
6. Nash, "Vietnam's Empty Forests."
7. "Viet Nam." *World Wildlife Fund*, n.d., worldwildlife.org. Accessed 7 Feb. 2025.
8. *Vietnam & Angkor Wat*. DK, 2015. 23.
9. Carl Engelking. "World's Second-Longest Insect Discovered in Vietnam." *Discover*, 30 Dec. 2014, discovermagazine.com. Accessed 7 Feb. 2025.
10. "Viet Nam."
11. *Vietnam & Angkor Wat*, 205.
12. Nash, "Vietnam's Empty Forests."
13. Nash, "Vietnam's Empty Forests."
14. *Vietnam & Angkor Wat*, 122.

CHAPTER 4. HISTORY

1. "Vietnam Country Profile." *BBC*, 23 Oct. 2024, bbc.com. Accessed 7 Feb. 2025.
2. *Worldmark Encyclopedia of Cultures and Daily Life: Asia & Oceania*. 3rd ed., Gale, 2017. 1064.
3. *Worldmark Encyclopedia*, 1302.
4. *Worldmark Encyclopedia*, 1064.
5. Brad Lendon. "My Lai: Ghosts in Another Vietnam Wall." *CNN*, 15 Mar. 2021, cnn.com. Accessed 7 Feb. 2025.
6. "Vietnam." *CIA World Factbook*, 5 Feb. 2025, cia.gov. Accessed 7 Feb. 2025.
7. *Worldmark Encyclopedia*, 1064.
8. "Vietnam's 'Bamboo Diplomacy' Shifts into Higher Gear." *Reuters*, 6 Mar. 2024, reuters.com. Accessed 7 Feb. 2025.

SOURCE **NOTES** CONTINUED

CHAPTER 5. PEOPLE AND CULTURE

1. "Vietnam." *CIA World Factbook*, 5 Feb. 2025, cia.gov. Accessed 7 Feb. 2025.
3. "Country Comparisons: Area." *CIA World Factbook*, n.d., cia.gov. Accessed 7 Feb. 2025.
4. "Vietnam."
5. "Vietnam."
6. "Vietnam."
7. Patricia M. Pelley. "Vietnam." *World Book Advanced*, n.d., worldbookonline.com. Accessed 7 Feb. 2025.
8. "Vietnam."
9. "Vietnam."
10. "Vietnam."

CHAPTER 6. POLITICS

1. *The Constitution of the Socialist Republic of Vietnam (2013): Unofficial Translation from Vietnamese by International IDEA*. International Institute for Democracy and Electoral Assistance, 2013, constitutionnet.org. Accessed 7 Feb. 2025.
2. "2022 Country Reports on Human Rights Practices: Vietnam." *US Department of State*, n.d., state.gov. Accessed 7 Feb. 2025.
3. James Pearson. "Fewer Independents Vie for Vietnam's Communist Party-Dominated Assembly." *Reuters*, 20 May 2021, reuters.com. Accessed 7 Feb. 2025.
4. "Vietnam." *CIA World Factbook*, 5 Feb. 2025, cia.gov. Accessed 7 Feb. 2025.
5. "Vietnam."
6. "Human Rights Practices: Vietnam."
7. Pearson. "Fewer Independents."
8. William S. Turley et al. "Vietnam." *Britannica*, 7 Feb. 2025, britannica.com. Accessed 7 Feb. 2025.
9. Huong Le Thu. "A Power Grab in Hanoi." *Foreign Affairs*, 9 Sept. 2024, foreignaffairs.com. Accessed 7 Feb. 2025.

CHAPTER 7. ECONOMICS

1. "Vietnam." *CIA World Factbook*, 5 Feb. 2025, cia.gov. Accessed 7 Feb. 2025.
2. "Vietnam."
3. "Banknotes & Coins: Typical Features." *State Bank of Vietnam*, n.d., sbv.gov.vn. Accessed 7 Feb. 2025.
4. "500,000 Vietnamese Dong to US Dollars—500,000 VND to USD Exchange Rate." *Exchange-Rates.org*, n.d., exchange-rates.org. Accessed 7 Feb. 2025.
5. William S. Turley et al. "Vietnam." *Britannica*, 7 Feb. 2025, britannica.com. Accessed 7 Feb. 2025.
6. M. Shahbandeh. "Principal Rice Exporting Countries Worldwide in 2024/2025." *Statista*, 22 Jan. 2025, statista.com. Accessed 24 Feb. 2025.
7. "Ho Chi Minh City Struggles to Implement Motorbike Emission Checks." *Asia News Network*, 27 Dec. 2021, asianews.network. Accessed 7 Feb. 2025.
8. "Vietnam."
9. "Vietnam."
10. John Yoon and Chau Doan. "Vietnamese Real Estate Tycoon Sentenced to Death in $12 Billion Fraud Case." *New York Times*, 11 Apr. 2024, nytimes.com. Accessed 7 Feb. 2025.
11. "Few Countries Are Better Placed Than Vietnam to Get Rich." *Gale Academic OneFile*, 23 Jan. 2024, go.gale.com. Accessed 7 Feb. 2025.

CHAPTER 8. VIETNAM TODAY

1. "Vietnamese Women's Participation in Labor Force High above Global Average: ILO." *Tuoi Tre News*, 8 Mar. 2021, tuoitrenews.vn. Accessed 7 Feb. 2025.
2. "How Nguyen Became the Most Common Vietnamese Surname in the World." *Saigoneer*, 26 Sept. 2017, saigoneer.com. Accessed 7 Feb. 2025.
3. "Vietnam." *CIA World Factbook*, 5 Feb. 2025, cia.gov. Accessed 7 Feb. 2025.
4. "Suoi Tien Cultural Theme Park." *Atlas Obscura*, 17 Oct. 2009, atlasobscura.com. Accessed 7 Feb. 2025.

INDEX

ABOUT THE **AUTHOR**

LIZ SONNEBORN

A graduate of Swarthmore College, Liz Sonneborn has written more than 100 books for young readers and adults on a wide variety of subjects. Her specialties include American history, world history, biography, women's studies, and African American studies. She is the author of more than a dozen books about the history and culture of various countries, such as Spain, Israel, Mexico, Canada, France, Iraq, Yemen, Kuwait, and Haiti. Her books also include *Vietnamese Americans*, *The Khmer Rouge*, and *Ancient China*.